Chronic Pain: Beyond The Meds

A groundbreaking non-drug approach to managing chronic pain

Dr. Jeremy Martin

xulon PRESS

Chronic Pain: Beyond The Meds
by Dr. Jeremy W. Martin

Printed in the United States of America

ISBN 9781619969384

www.xulonpress.com

A special thanks for my family for allowing me the time to write, practice, consult, attend class and go to seminars so that I may be a blessing to the people who need me. As always, thanks goes to God for allowing me to do what I do and for blessing me and my family. I also want to thank the people and healthcare providers who say you cannot really help people with chronic conditions. You make me want to learn more and become a better healthcare practitioner. Also, a special thanks to those who bought the previous book about dealing with ADHD.

Table of Contents

Chapter 1: Scope of the Problem 9

Chapter 2: The Causes.. 31

Chapter 3: The Symptoms 73

Chapter 4: Diagnosis/Labels/Expectations 97

Chapter 5: The Normal Treatments...................................... 109

Chapter 6: What Makes Our Program Different 129

Chapter 7: What It Takes.. 137

Chapter 1:

Scope of the Problem

Chapter 1:

Scope of the Problem

"The doctor of the future will give no medicine, but will interest his patients in the care of the human frame, in diet, and in the cause and prevention of disease."

–Thomas Edison

I love that quote from Thomas Edison. I believe future is here. I believe Edison's future is now. The challenge is finding a contemporary doctor, a doctor of today. The contemporary doctor of today does interest his patients in the care of the human frame (including the brain, spine and nervous system). The contemporary doctor of today does interest his patient in what they are putting in their body (including food, drugs, and supplements). The contemporary doctor of today does interest his patients in the cause and prevention of disease (including genetics, environment, exercise, autoimmunity, and inflammation). It is imperative for people experiencing chronic pain to find a healthcare practitioner who is contemporary. Contemporary in this setting refers to a healthcare practitioner who stays informed of the current literature, who stays on top of the current techniques for helping people get well, and is always willing to change in an effort to help his patients in the greatest possible way.

Chronic pain is overwhelming our adult population. It is very disheartening to consider the health of the senior and adult population of the United States. The older we get as an American, the sicker we get on average. A recent article in the Wall Street Journal, written in November of 2011, reports that one hundred and sixteen million American adults (roughly one third of the population) deal with chronic pain. The Wall Street Journal goes on to report that the Institute of Medicine found in July of 2011 that Many of the people dealing with chronic pain are treated "inadequately". I believe the word inadequate could be thought of as not contemporary or not of today's time. That is a lot of cases not being handled well. I am going to help you learn a better way.

One third of the adult population in the United States is enormous. Those are just the reported cases. There are more. It is very likely that if you are old enough, you know someone experiencing some type chronic pain syndrome. Even though it is reported that the average American is living longer, I believe I will make the case that the quality of life of the average American is becoming poorer and poorer. I do not believe we have the quality of life in this country that we enjoyed in the past. I do not like to hear the reports of so many other countries are enjoying a better quality of health than we are.

So we know there are many millions of people that are reported living in the United States with severe pain. We know these are just the cases that have been identified and diagnosed. Many more people are on their way to dealing with chronic pain as they get older. The cause and prevention of chronic pain are very poorly understood by most mainstream healthcare providers as well as alternative healthcare providers. The proper training is often just not there. What is worse is that the majority of mainstream healthcare providers try to treat chronic conditions in the same manor as they would treat acute situations. It is just not working. I believe that by the time you finish reading this book you will understand many of the reasons behind chronic pain and that you will understand the importance and the mechanics behind a drug free care program. As a side note, acute health situations are usually short term conditions that may or may not be life threatening. Chronic health situations are usually longer in duration (most lasting at least six months). The life threatening nature of chronic conditions usually comes from the body shutting down after a long term assault on the systems of the body. Certainly not all health conditions are life threatening, but some of the conditions involving chronic pain can be.

I sat down and wrote this book for many reasons. The first

reason is that I firmly believe we have one of the finest chronic pain management systems in the world today. We have combined Functional Neurology, Functional Nutrition, brainmapping and Neurointegration. The second reason for this book is to answer many of the questions that we receive on a regular basis. Almost every paragraph in this book deals with a question that I regularly receive. I hope that this book spreads the information that people are looking for. The last and probably the most important reason for this book is to provide hope for the sufferer of chronic pain as well as their family and friends. The overwhelming success of my last book, <u>ADHD: Beyond The Meds</u>, also let me know that the public is interested in new ways to deal with their health. Many of the answers that people seek are out there. Many of the answer do not come from the places people are looking.

Many of the people living with chronic pain feel like they are often misunderstood by those closest too them. I unfortunately see this very frequently. People often do not understand how an adult could be in such a great deal of pain. Both sides often feel a sense of betrayal. This is a very sad situation. We see this over in over in at least half of the chronic pain cases we manage. It is very often the case in life that if an individual has not experienced a certain situation for themselves, he or she is unable to understand or believe a person who is experiencing chronic pain. Such is the case with chronic pain.

A great deal of sufferers of chronic pain do not feel like their health care providers understand their situation either. Quite frankly, I do not think that many of them do understand. I hear this from almost every chronic pain patient that we see. Most of them say that if their healthcare provider cannot figure out the cause they want to tell the patient they must be depressed. Just because a doctor cannot figure out the cause of the problem does not mean the patient is making up the symptoms. Make sure you remember that for yourself and your family. Having symptoms that a group of healthcare providers cannot figure out does not necessarily make you a depressed person. It has gotten to where over ninety percent of the chronic pain patients we see are on some type of antidepressant and most have no idea why.

Unfortunately the current healthcare system really does not allow healthcare providers to spend the amount of time required for these patients and advanced training for chronic pain is rarely encouraged. The closer and closer we are getting to socialized medicine, the worse the system is getting. So many Americans are really unaware of how bad our system is actually getting. Patients are so much more than a number on an insurance card. Adults and seniors living with chronic pain need to be treated like individuals. I am holding out hope not as a healthcare provider, but as an American, that the socialized medicine does not fully catch on here.

People with chronic pain need to demand the proper testing and the proper care. First, they have to learn what proper care and proper testing consists of. I believe this book will help a great deal with that challenge. The days of totally relying on a healthcare provider to look out for your best interests are over. In many cases those healthcare providers are restricted by insurance companies at what they can do for a person. A person must learn as much as they can about how their body works and what their body needs to function at its highest levels.

Even worse for me than the adult situation, is the situation involving young people and chronic pain. It was recently reported that chronic pain is becoming a much more common complaint in children. The article went on to quote a recent pain journal in saying "Results of this review indicate that persistent and recurrent chronic pain is overwhelmingly prevalent in children and adolescents and should be recognized as a major health concern in this population" (Buffalo News December 27, 2011). The current statistics from the Kaiser Health Foundation found the average annual prescription for children is now almost four prescriptions per child ages zero to eighteen (Mercola July 2, 2011). We have to start looking for answers in different places. The old way of dealing with pain is just not working. The old way is an over-dependence on drugs. Drugs are very rarely the long term answer to any health problem. We can no longer hope to continue drugging the problem away.

Chronic pain is such a huge problem. So many people feel so hopeless. Chronic pain is another example of how the drugs only work on a limited basis. I am not anti-drug. That is very important for me to state. I am anti-the easy way out. We have become far too dependent on medications to minimize our pain. So many healthcare providers use these drugs as their only tool for pain relief. There is no doubt that there are cases that the drugs are necessary. It is just so how out of hand it has gotten. Most cases of chronic pain can be minimized and some even corrected without the use of these dangerous medications. In fact, in many cases the chronic pain can be avoided with taking the proper actions.

Many of the people we work with are able to come off their medications or greatly reduce the amount of medications they are currently taking. The side effects of many of these drugs have just become too much. A recent article on Mercola.com reported the average drug label lists over seventy side effects with some drugs listing up to five hundred twenty five reactions! The article went on to state that more than seven hundred thousand people visit emergency rooms in the United States each year as a result of a drug reaction. The Center for Disease Control recently issued a statement that prescription drugs kill more people than the illegal drugs. Think about that. My generation grew up hearing just say no to illegal drugs. Maybe we should say no to the legal drugs more often.

We have become too dependent on medications for our health and the health of our children. The drugs are not working well for many chronic conditions. The drugs have their place. I am glad the drugs are available in acute situations. In life and death situations, traditional healthcare typically does a very good job. It is the chronic cases that people are losing hope in their healthcare providers. It is the chronic cases that more and more drugs are added to the care program in some attempt to achieve some form of results.

The ball is being dropped over and over in these chronic cases. I am amazed at the amount of chronic pain patients that are on muscle relaxer, painkillers, antidepressants, and even anti-seizure medications. It gets to where the patients and the doctors forget why the patient is on all of the pills. Most of the patients we see cannot tell me why they are taking the drugs they are taking and almost none of these patients have been told about any of the potential side effects of these medications. The doctors really need to be more transparent with their patients. People should be told why they are on a drug and what the potential side effects are. Doctors of all kinds need to stop being so heavily influenced by the pharmaceutical industry. A recent report found that in 2010, twelve pharmaceutical companies paid seven hundred sixty million dollars to physicians and other health care providers for various reasons (Mercola Nov 24, 2011). If we are going to fully trust our healthcare providers, they are going to have to quit taking kickbacks from the pharmaceutical industry.

In the vast majority of chronic cases, I do not believe the drugs are not working in the manner attended. In many cases, the drugs are very dangerous. Again, most people are unaware of the danger. A study published in the Journal of the American Medical Association reported one hundred six thousand people die and two million two hundred thousand are injured each year by adverse reactions to prescription drugs (Null, 2010). In his book <u>Death By Medicine</u>, Phd Gary Null reports that seven hundred eighty three thousand nine hundred eighty six people die in the United States each year from conventional medical mistakes. That is the equivalent of six jumbo jets crashing every day (Null, 2010). Six jumbo jet every day! Why do we not hear this more on the news? This should be a fact that every American knows. We need to make better choices with regards to our health. We need to stay better informed and really watch who we get our information from. We need to care more.

There is a better way. In many cases there is a non-drug way to manage chronic pain. Some people find that very hard to believe. Some people have such poor functioning brains and nervous systems, the are unable to really believe anything. I see this quite often. These people are so sick they are

Chronic Pain: Beyond The Meds

unable to make the right decision. The frontal lobe of the brain is the area of the brain that allows us to make choices. It is this part of the brain that is often compromised in chronic pain scenarios. It is very sad to see people that are unable to really understand the choices there are in healthcare. That is where family and friends are needed to help some of these chronic pain patients realize they have choices.

The great part about our chronic pain management program is that it is not faith based. You do not have to believe you are going to get better to get results. I am fortunate enough to get to witness it on a daily basis. Give the body what it needs and very good things happen. Give the body what it needs and healing is possible. There is an incredible design to our body and I feel very fortunate to get to deal with that design.

Our bodies require proper fuel and proper activation to survive. Without proper fuel and activation, dysfunction and disease occur. Those are actually the core tenants of Functional Neurology. Functional Neurology is the healthcare system created by Dr. Ted Carrick of The Carrick Institute. I encourage all healthcare providers to look up Dr. Carrick and see what he has to say about health. The activation of our nervous system makes all the difference in the world. I believe I will make a very compelling case for that point of view during the course of this book. A quick fix for chronic health problems rarely exists. I am constantly amazed at the mass quantities of drugs many of the patients that come into my office are frequently on.

The average American citizen is on more than twelve medications (Mercola, December 2008). The average annual prescription rate for seniors aged sixty five and over is more than thirty one prescriptions (Mercola, July 2011). That is an astounding number. Think about that. That is the average. I am not on any medications. Many of my patients are not on any medications. That means there are people out there on over thirty medications for our citizens to average over eleven. It saddens me to hear how many seniors and middle aged adults are constantly visiting all types of doctors offices looking for answers on such a frequent basis.

I have seen patients on as many as thirty medications. Seniors are especially becoming over-dependant on these drugs. Dr Gordon Schiff of the Women's Hospital in Boston says this problem is a "product of a medical system that offers little in the way of disease prevention and non-drug alternatives, and is challenged to think beyond drugs when a person comes in with a medical complaint." Do you really believe that many chemicals are needed in our bodies to produce proper function? Do you believe that people are in pain because of a lack of drugs in their body?

Many people suffering with chronic pain deal with other chronic health issues such as insomnia, anxiety, irritable bowel syndrome, headaches, poor memory, fatigue, poor cognition/poor thinking, high blood pressure, as well as many other symptoms. I have personally dealt with irritable bowel syndrome. That was some of the worst pain I have ever experienced. I believe that beating Irritable Bowel Syndrome has given me a unique perspective in dealing with chronic pain. I believe that having great success with many chronic pain patients has given me reason to write this book. We are able to achieve results in patients who have given up hope.

Many people suffering with chronic pain think drugs are their only choice. Many people are told drugs are their only choice. I was told there was no choice for me when I experienced Irritable Bowel Syndrome. In fact, at twenty years old, I was told that the cause for my Irritable Bowel Syndrome was that my body was getting older. That left me very little hope. Many think there is no hope. I am here to tell them there is hope. I am here to tell them they have choices. There are many non-drug choices. We have been very successful helping people avoid drugs and surgeries over the years. We have been successful in changing lives of those people in pain.

As I mentioned before, one of the saddest and most common situations that we see with chronic pain is the situation in which the loved ones of the person in pain do not understand or believe that the degree of pain the individual suffers from. If you are not dealing with the pain yourself, it is a very difficult thing to understand. This often brings feelings

26

of hopelessness and despair. Many of the people we help with chronic pain feel beaten down by family, friends and co-workers. This often can be a cause of anxiety or depression for the chronic pain sufferer. So many of these people feel isolated from their friends and family. Many of the patients we see do not tell their friends and family the degree of their health problems. This problem is usually treated with antidepressants added to the drug cocktail.

There are quite a few different types of chronic pain. I personally am not big on spending too much time trying to name the disease or chronic pain syndrome. I want to see what the causative factors are and get to addressing those factors. In my office ninety nine percent of our effort is to find the cause of the problem, not the name. But in this age of healthcare we should at least talk about what some of these chronic pain problems are called. Examples of some of the chronic pain syndromes include fibromyalgia, migraine headaches, tension headaches, cluster headaches, trigeminal neuralgia, peripheral neuropathy, temporo-mandibular joint dysfunction (TMJ), chronic low back pain, chronic neck pain, chronic thoracic pain, chronic disc problems, spinal stenosis, irritable bowel syndrome, Crohn's disease, diabetic neuropathy, lupus, rheumatoid arthritis, and gout.

Lets discuss fibromyalgia. Fibromyalgia is a very misunderstood diagnosis. I will admit that for many years I doubted that people could really hurt that bad for no apparent reason. Most healthcare providers just do not have the proper training to help those people suffering with fibromyalgia. It is just not commonly taught. Many patients are given this catchall phrase when frustrated healthcare providers no longer know what to do with their chronic pain patients. I see this on a very regular basis. Fibromyalgia is a very real condition. With the right type of care, fibromyalgia patients can achieve very real results. By the way, my definition of real results are patients reporting decreases of pain levels by fifty percent or more. Always know what the goal of your healthcare provider is for you and your case. If I accept a case, I expect fifty to one hundred percent change.

Fibromyalgia is very hard to manage without the proper tools. Many healthcare practitioners do not want to deal with this problem. I hear this more and more. I have really grown to enjoy working with this group. We have been very successful dealing with the people with fibromyalgia. Only in the last five to six years of practice have the really good results come though. This was after discovering that the problem was not at the site of pain. Understanding the mechanisms that are involved is of upmost importance. If the healthcare provider does not understand that the vast majority of these people have hyper functioning brains and nervous systems, the results will almost always be limited. The term hyper means that certain parts of the brain are often over-firing. This over-firing is often the chief causative factor of pain.

The good news is that there is hope for these people in pain. I get to see it on a daily basis. Lives are changed and I believe many lives are saved. A life with no, or just minimal drugs, is so much easier on our liver and kidneys. Many patients we work with are able to come off their drugs and the others are able to greatly reduce the drugs that they are taking on our program. Many are able to understand the cause of their condition for the first time. The diagnosis can be useful, but finding the cause of the problem is so much better for the patient and the doctor.

I do believe the diagnosis of fibromyalgia is overused by healthcare practitioners. More than half of the people initially coming to see us for this do not actually have what they have been diagnosed with. Many, many people who think they have fibromyalgia actually have a different chronic pain syndrome. Fibromyalgia has unfortunately become a catchall diagnosis when a doctor cannot figure out what to do with a patient. Quite frankly, I do not believe that naming the problem the patient has, is nearly important as finding the cause of the pain. I believe that finding the site or sites of dysfunction is of utmost importance.

Chapter 2:

The Causes

Chapter 2:

The Causes

"A long habit of not thinking a thing wrong gives it a super-
ficial appearance of being right."

–Thomas Paine

The practice of focusing on the symptoms only in a chronic pain scenario has to change. This has been the standard operating procedure of far too many healthcare providers in this country. Why continue to add drugs to the patient's care program without understanding the nature and ultimate cause of the problem. Healthcare providers have to start looking more into the causative factors involved in these chronic pain situations. I am not sure how much value there is in naming a patient's condition without finding out what is causing the condition.

Here is a very important point to make. I want you to really get this. This is a new concept to many people suffering with chronic pain. This is a new point for some healthcare providers. Here is the big point. **Each chronic pain case if different.** Let me say that again to really drive home this point. Each chronic pain case is different. Some very different. Some cases are more neurologically driven (meaning driven by dysfunction of the nervous system). Some cases are more metabolically drive (meaning driven by dysfunction of the blood). Some cases are driven more by the immune system. Some cases are driven by the food a person puts into their body. Some cases are even driven by infections and parasites. Some cases are more genetically driven. Some cases are more environmentally driven. Some cases are more hormonally driven. The key is to understand is that individuals have individual problems and causes. Rarely in life is there a one size fits all solution. As a side note I will say that family members sometimes end up having a like cause though, especially autoimmune cases.

There is no one cause and no one catch all cure for chronic pain. Putting a label on your problem does not make you the same as the other chronic pain sufferers with that label. I have found that the need to put a label on a person's problem usually exists for the sake of getting paid by insurance companies. Labels do not often equate to a effective treatment. No matter what the late night infomercials or the latest multilevel marketing supplement company says or the latest drug advertisement says, a magic silver bullet does not exist. I wish they did work. Cookie-cutter approaches do not work well, including medications. That is a big statement for some to handle. Just because you were given a specific diagnosis does not mean that the mechanisms of your problem are truly understood. Think about the people you know with not just chronic pain, but any chronic condition. How many of them are getting better? How many of them are adding more and more drugs to their care program on a regular basis?

It seems that it has become common practice lately among

healthcare providers to let people continue to become worse and worse until the patient presents enough symptoms that a disorder or disease can be put upon the patient. I cannot tell you how much we are seeing this practice lately. I wish more providers focused on the patient outcome more than the diagnosis. Labels are more for insurance companies and doctors than for patients. We recently had a patient who had been to another healthcare provider who wanted the patient's symptoms to get worse before he tried to help her. I will never understand that type of thinking. Why wait for someone to deteriorate before you try to help them? We are for helping each and every patient at the place they are currently at.

Healthcare providers should always try to look for ways to help the patient not continue to get worse. This is very important in chronic conditions. Waiting for enough tissue to have destruction so that the disease process can be named is a very big mistake. This type of thinking has to be changed. So often our healthcare providers are limited in what they can do until a person fits into a diagnosis code for a insurance company.

Do not let any doctor tell you to wait until you get worse to try to figure out what is wrong with you.

Remember, there is no magic silver bullet. You have to be very care of what you put in your body. Exotic fruit drinks or fruit pills have become very popular lately. I happen to like many of them. Many of these fruit juices, full of antioxidants, may good for some people and not so good for other people. Make sure you read this next part. Certain antioxidants have been found to actually drive or make autoimmune conditions worse. In case you do not know, autoimmune conditions are a situation that the body attacks itself for a variety of different reasons. Please do not think that if a fruit is from a place that you have never heard of that it must be good for you. One antioxidant that I believe to be safe, regardless of auto-immune issues, is glutathione. Learn all that you can about glutathione.

Without getting into too much detail, we all have a immune system that has different parts called the Th1 and the Th2 system. Th stands for t helper. T cells make up a very important part of the overall immune system. The Th1 and Th2 systems of the immune system are driven or increased by different things. There should be a balance between the two systems. When there is not a proper balance of these system, autoimmune attacks can occur. There was a paper published by the University of Oregon's Health and Science department that reported that "there is a growing body of evidence supporting a link between cytokines and somatic complaints" (Thompson and Barkhuizen, 2003). Another paper in 2011 out of the Australian National University stated "There is also evidence that CFS patients have a relative immunodeficiency that predisposes to poor early control of infection that leads to chronic inflammatory responses to infectious insults" (Arnett et al, 2011).

Dysfunction of the immune system is very common in people with chronic pain. Georgetown University Medical Center published a report in 2005 that stated "In patients with CFS (Chronic Fatigue Syndrome), there appears to be a fundamental dysfunction of the neuroendocrine-immunological system with deficiencies of immunological and neurological function" (Bellanti et al, 2005). It is important to find the cause of the pain and to not shoot blindly in the dark in an attempt to gain relief. Knowing what you are dealing with is of utmost importance and autoimmunity is becoming a bigger and bigger problem on a yearly basis.

I have said this many times already, but I do not want you to miss this point. Each person is different and each person with chronic pain can be very different. It is very important to identify the unique nature of each person's situation. Some people have more metabolic/autoimmune components and other people have more neurologic/brain based components. Many of these people deal with improper toxin levels. Toxicity can play a big role in chronic pain. The cause of the pain is of upmost importance. The cause of the pain is so much more important than the diagnosis.

Metabolic/autoimmune components can be measured through blood testing, saliva testing, and stool testing. It is vital your practitioner use the right form of testing in these cases because many false negatives are found with improper testing. False negatives occur when the testing one uses is not sensitive enough and falsely tells a doctor nothing is wrong. Some of the best laboratory testing has become available very recently. We see this very often with food reactivity testing. It is now generally well accepted that food can cause different reactions in the body. We know that food can cause immune reactions in some people. It is important that more healthcare providers understand the link between the immune system, the nervous system and chronic pain.

Neurological/brain based components can be measured through computerized quantative EEG (QEEG) brain mapping and a functional neurological examination. The QEEG testing involves the use of electrodes to acquire the brainwave activity. That activity is then measured against a normative database. A functional neurological evaluation looks at the motor output of the person's nervous system and compare that to the normal or expected responses. Knowing what the individual's nervous system is doing is imperative. We would not get the excellent results we routinely get with chronic pain patients without this information. This information is almost always missed among more mainstream healthcare providers. A person does not have to have a disease process going on to have dysfunction of the nervous system. In fact, I think it would be in the patient's best interest to try to deal with this dysfunction before it becomes a disease process.

The vast majority of chronic pain sufferers are dealing with functional neurological problems. Functional neurological problems basically mean neurological problems that are not the result of an ablative lesion, such as a tumor or a stroke. Functional neurology can also mean the management of a neurological condition without the use of drugs or surgery. Most chronic pain sufferers have improper levels of brain waves in the cortex of the brain (the upper portion of the brain) and/or have an overactive upper brainstem (under the cortex). That statement is a generalization, but it happens to be true in approximately ninety percent of the chronic pain cases I have dealt with to some degree.

The brain cerebrum is the top of the brain that most people think of when someone refers to the brain. It is the part with all of the folds and crevices. Beneath the brain cerebrum is the brainstem. The brainstem is incredibly important in chronic pain. The upper portion of the brainstem is called the mesencephalon. A high percentage of the people with chronic pain that we deal with have over firing mesencephalons. Most patients have never heard the word mesencephalon. It is very important to balance these areas of the brain if long term relief and management of chronic stress is to take place. This is often able to be done without drugs or surgery. We will get to the how later in the book.

Another part of the brain that is often involved in chronic pain is called the cerebellum. The cerebellum is located in the posterior lower part of the brain. The cerebellum is important for a wide variety of body functions. This area plays a large role in the integration of sensory information, which is a chief problem in many chronic pain cases. As Dr. Beck puts it in his book, Functional Neurology for Practitioners of Manual

Therapy, "the cerebellum and vestibular systems also play a role in the integration of sensory information that is essential for generating appropriate responses to environmental stimuli and for a variety of other functions including constructing a perception of ourselves in the universe; controlling muscle movement; maintaining balance; maintaining internal organ and blood flow functionality; maintaining cortical arousal; and developing active plasticity in neural networks which allow environmental conditioning to occur" (Beck,2008). A proper functional neurological evaluation of the cerebellum is important to see if there is dysfunction. I would strongly encourage healthcare provider unfamiliar with functional neurology to study Dr. Beck's textbook.

We know that our physical body works by electrical and chemical properties. We can measure the electrical portion by means of QEEG. This type of monitoring involves small leads that are attached to specific portions of the head that correspond to specific areas of the brain. QEEG monitoring has been around for a long time. The military, big business, researchers, doctors of all kinds and sporting teams are currently making use of QEEG. The monitoring of brainwaves have been greatly refined and improved upon over the years. It is one of the greatest tools I have in my practice to assess function of the brain.

In 1875, Richard Caton discovered fluctuations in the brain's electrical activity following mental activity (Demos, 2004). Researchers have been looking at brain waves for over 135 years. In the 1930s, Edgar Adrian and BHC Matthews showed brainwave patterns could be modified by specific frequencies of light (Demos, 2004). This discovery opened the door for use of EEG technology as treatment. This is often a major portion of my treatment protocol. People with overactive motor/sensory strips, located on the top of the brain between the ears, often perceive pain more intensely than they should. This of course is a huge generalization about people with chronic pain and that is why we perform a brain map and see the situation of the individual's brain.

Next, lets discuss the thyroid. Many people with chronic

pain syndromes have thyroid dysfunction. The thyroid gland is found about three quarters of the way down on a person's neck. Again, naming the dysfunction is not as important for me as knowing that the dysfunction exists. This can be checked with proper blood testing. Unfortunately, the proper testing is rarely done anymore within the confines of the insurance model of healthcare outside the offices of endocrinologists. The thyroid gland is a very important hormone producing tissue in our body that is located in the neck region. In fact, every cell in the body has receptor sites for thyroid hormones. That is an amazing fact. Every cell in our body may have the potential to interact with thyroid hormones.

Thyroid hormones play many very important roles in the body such as: immune system modulators, inflammatory mediation (we know inflammation very often has a large role in chronic pain issue), influences the integrity of the tight junctions of the gastrointestinal barrier system (which has the potential for the development of leaky gut syndrome), influences microglia cells and neuronal neurotransmitters, and

45

promotes an overall healthy brain.

Thyroid dysfunction can cause a tremendous decrease in energy levels (which we often see with chronic pain), alterations in mental function and mood, and gastrointestinal problems. The clinical symptoms associated with hypothyroidism include: fatigue, depression, weight gain, lack of motivation, poor recovery from injuries and workouts, and constipation. The clinical signs include: hair thinning, hair loss, swelling, puffy face, dry skin and obesity. Every case is different. Some chronic pain patients have one of the above problems and some have them all.

Many of the thyroid problems have an autoimmune component. The thyroid gland is the most common site of an autoimmune attack. This is known as Hashimoto's Disease. Hashimoto's Disease is becoming more and more common in the United States. This disease is believed to be the most prevalent autoimmune disorder in the United States (Kharrazian, 2009). One study found that between 7-8 percent of the U.S. population have antibodies against their thyroid. We have found this situation with many of our chronic pain sufferers. This occurs with the presence of a high TSH marker in the blood with the presence of thyroid antibodies high in the blood. Medication often has to be used in the cases of patients with Hashimoto's disease. We will discuss this more when we get to the part of the book that deals with what your next steps should be.

The thyroid gland is very susceptible to, like many other tissues in our body, to environmental factors, to medications and to hormones. Medications that can really affect they thyroid include: anti-inflammatories, antibiotics, antidepressants, diabetic medications, hypertensive medications, pain medications, antacids, and cholesterol lowering drugs. The hormones that affect the thyroid include: estrogens, progesterone, cortisol and testosterone. I hope I have made the case for the importance of proper thyroid function.

Immune dysregulation is becoming a larger issue each year. The Washington Post reported on March 4, 2008 that experts estimate that many immune system diseases (of which there are many) have doubled, tripled or even quadrupled in the last few decades. The diseases associated with autoimmunity are mainly on the rise in highly developed countries in Europe and North America. There is a strong correlation between development in countries and the rise of autoimmune disease. I believe autoimmunity is very much linked to environmental factors.

Autoimmunity is starting to receive the attention that it deserves in healthcare. It is very important to see if there is an autoimmune component occurring with chronic pain patients. Very often that is the case. Naming the autoimmune disease is not as important as finding the underlying cause. We have already mentioned the autoimmune thyroid component. It is very important to try to catch an autoimmune issues as early as possible when dealing with chronic pain. Whatever type of healthcare provider you choose to work with, I would strongly encourage you and you doctor to rule out any immune dysfunction.

Glucose and iron dysfunction are also common. These

are two of the chief metabolic factors we mentioned earlier. Glucose and iron are essential for fuel delivery. Glucose is basically the sugar that our body uses for fuel. We do not necessarily always see diabetes, hypoglycemia or anemia, but we often see numbers that are not optimal. Improper glucose delivery ultimately affects energy production in the body. Improper iron levels can affect the amount of oxygen that can be delivered to different areas of the body. We often look at lab numbers from a functional model instead of a disease state mode. The functional numbers are usually much more conservative and give an individual the best chance at intervention before a disease process develops. Optimal numbers are important regarding glucose and iron concerning brain function. Remember the cause of dysfunction is much more important than the names.

Overactive brain sensory association areas are very common with chronic pain. I mentioned before that one causative factor often found is an over-activated cerebral area. Midway on our scalp, between our ears, is where the sensory and motor strip is located. People in the neurofeedback world call this area C3/C4. We often find over-activation of beta and/or alpha waves in this area. We also often find over-activation of the frontal lobes of the brain in chronic pain. People in the neurofeedback world call this area F3/F4. Beta and alpha waves are the faster brainwaves and theta and delta are the slower brainwaves. It is important for proper brain health that these waves be in proper ratios. These waves can be monitored, recorded and trained to stay at proper levels with neurofeedback.

Neurofeedback is a computerized training of the brainwaves, using EEG leads, while the individual watches a movie or listens to music. Neurointegration takes it one step further and uses blinking glasses of different colors to help suggest to the brain what its proper brainwave patterns should be. I have found this to be highly useful in helping those with chronic pain. In fact, I have found this type of training to be highly effective in the management of insomnia, anxiety, neurobehavioral disorders of childhood as well. I really appreciate the statement by Dr. Frank Duffy, a Harvard trained neurologist, who stated, "In my opinion, if any medication had demonstrated such a wide spectrum of efficacy it would be universally accepted and widely used."

It is also very important to see if there is a functional brainstem problem. This problem can often be found on a functional neurological examination. The upper portion of the brainstem is called the mesencephalon. The mesencephalon is often referred to as the midbrain. There is often mesencephalic dysfunction in chronic pain syndromes. Many times the activity of this portion of the nervous system can be determined by watching the activity of the eyes. The eyes are the window to the brain. The mesencephalon can be dampened with very specific brain based therapies which slow this system down. We will often have the patient do specific breathing exercises, wear special colored glasses and do eye exercises in this process. Just doing this part alone often helps those dealing with chronic pain.

Cortisol dysfunction is common in a very high percentage

of chronic pain sufferers. Many people correlate cortisol as being a bad thing. This is definitely not the case. Cortisol is a very important substance for the normal operations of our body. We know that chronically high levels of cortisol can literally destroy very important areas of the brain. One area in particular that is sensitive to cortisol dysfunction is called the hippocampus. The hippocampus is believed to be very important for conscious memory and learning. Memory and the ability to learn new things is often compromised in people with chronic pain.

Cortisol is a hormone made by our adrenal glands, which sit on top of our kidneys, that is designed to maintain proper glucose levels in the body. This hormone is an especially big player in the management of chronic pain. We are finding more and more problems with cortisol, especially as people get older. Cortisol checks are important for everyone with chronic pain or any type of chronic stress. It is rare to find someone with a chronic pain problem who does not have a cortisol problem. Cortisol function is a very big deal. In fact, I would recommend a proper cortisol check for everyone over the age of thirty five on a yearly basis.

Some of the symptoms of impaired adrenal glands are: low body temperature, weakness, hair loss, nervousness, difficulty building muscle, irritability, depression, apprehension, hypoglycemia, inability to concentrate, excessive hunger, confusion, indigestion, poor memory, frustration, diarrhea/constipation, autoimmunity, lightheadedness, palpitations dizziness, poor resistance to infections, low blood pressure, insomnia, food allergies, food cravings, dry skin, and headaches.

So it is important to understand that cortisol is not a bad thing. Proper cortisol function is actually a very good thing. Cortisol regulates our glucose, which is important for literally every aspect of our body's function. Improper cortisol regulation by the body is a bad thing. This often occurs after major life stressors. I have heard it said that the three biggest stressors in a persons life are dealing with the death of a loved on, getting a divorce, and moving from their home. Constant relatively minor stressors can also add up over a period of time as well.

The cortisol levels are very easily tested. It is very important to do this the correct way, as there are many choices with the testing. We like looking at not only the levels of cortisol, but the overall pattern throughout the day. Cortisol production should be high in the morning and low in the evening. That pattern is very important to maintain.

There are many non-drug options if dysfunction exists. Once a healthcare provider finds the pattern of dysfunction, the treatment protocols are often pretty black and white. Causes of cortisol dysfunction include: anger, fear, worry, anxiety, depression, guilt physical strain, mental strain, sleep deprivation, going to sleep late, injury, inflammation, infection, pain, extreme temperatures, toxin exposure, malabsorption, maldigestion, hypoglycemia, and nutritional deficiencies. I hope we have made a good case for proper functioning adrenal glands.

Along with checking the cortisol levels, we also look at secretory IgA levels. Wikipedia states, "In its secretory form,

IgA is the main immunoglobulin found in mucous secretions, including tears, saliva, colostrum and secretions from the genitourinary tract, gastrointestinal tract, prostate and respiratory epithelium." The fact is that the majority of our immune system is found in our gut. By monitoring SIgA levels we can monitor the level of immune function. SIgA is thought to be one of the first lines of defense against pathogens or foreign invaders to the body. Depression of this marker can often mean the individual is more susceptible to allergies, infections, and chronic disease. This is very often an area we see a deficit in when dealing with people in chronic pain. More and more doctors are catching on to this and I am very happy to see this trend.

We often find what is called Leaky Gut Syndrome in individuals dealing with pain. This syndrome occurs when the tight junctions of your gastrointestinal system, that should remain impermeable, become loose or permeable to substances that are otherwise unable to pass through the barrier system. This loosening of the inner workings of the gastrointestinal system can come after chronic stress, chronic infection or even medication usage. Leaky Gut Syndrome can cause different things to be in your bloodstream that should not be there. The body will often find these item to be pathogens and will cause an autoimmune attack. The autoimmune attack raises cytokine levels, which are described as the messenger system of the immune system, and cause further destruction of the tight junctions of the intestines. There is very good testing available to find out if a person has Leaky Gut Syndrome.

Leaky guts can often be corrected using the correct nutritional protocols to restore the tight junctions of the stomach and small intestine. The traditional test for leaky gut syndrome has been around for many years. Just recently, there have been very important advances made in the testing for this problem. This is especially important in those pain syndromes with an autoimmune factor. Recently leaky gut syndrome has also been linked with depression. We know that depression is often a cofactor of chronic pain syndromes. It is a very sad fact that most healthcare providers miss the importance of proper gut health.

We also often find that people with chronic pain have chronic bacterial infections or even parasites. It is very important to have this tested in chronic situations. A research paper in 2008 stated "Infections and vaccinations have also been linked to the pathogenesis of fibromyalgia" (Baio et al, 2008). Some people have yeast overgrowth and some even have issues with mold. Many of these infections can go unnoticed for many months or even years. Far too many mainstream healthcare providers overlook this aspect of chronic pain when the testing is so simple. Stool samples can be tested to find if this is the case.

The most common infection we find is what is called h. pylori. This organism causes a large amount of infections all over the world. The best test for h. pylori is actually a breath test to see if you are infected. The breath test measures the amount of urea, which is waste product, that the organism puts off. This test has become very affordable over the last few years. It was not that long ago that I remember this test being around one thousand dollars. Now I believe it is available for around one hundred dollars. I highly recommend getting this test for people dealing with chronic pain. Many people find that they can ward off these h. pylori infections with use of probiotics. A recent study out of Wayne State University found that probiotics "may especially be helpful in patients with recurrent H. pylori infection and a history of gastrointestinal adverse effects with antibiotics" (Wilhem, Johnson, and Kale-Pradhan, 2011).

Toxins can also play a major role in the understanding and management of chronic pain syndromes. The bottom line is that none of us can totally get away from the toxins. Many healthcare providers and chronic pain sufferers really miss this issue. Our food, our water and our overall environment is changing for the worse on a daily basis. Our food is not what it once was and often not what we think it is. Start reading what you are putting in your body and the bodies of your family members. It makes a big difference.

New reports are coming our on a monthly basis on the

devastating hit our environment is taking. Over 80,000 chemicals have been introduced into our society since 1900, and fewer than 600 have been safety tested (Hyman, 2009). The state of our environment is getting worse by the day. We are constantly bombarded with unsafe chemicals. Our brain, our musculoskeletal system and our hormone producing tissues are especially susceptible to environmental toxins. I have heard several people say we are living in a sea of toxins. I fully agree with that statement.

More and more pesticides are being used on our fruits and vegetables. The average person in the United States who eats conventionally grown fruits and vegetables consumes approximately one gallon of pesticides and herbicides each year (Hyman, 2009). It is amazing to think of poison in such terms. It is very important to recognize the issue with pesticides and try to limit exposure. Fresh, healthy food is very important for everyone. It is a must when dealing with chronic pain.

Lets now look at sleep. People are not getting enough sleep. This is big. We heal and regenerate when we sleep. I do not believe I have seen a chronic pain patient who reported that they slept well. When a person does not sleep well, they do not regenerate and heal properly. The average adult needs seven to eight hours of sleep per night. The quality of sleep is just as important as the quantity of sleep. The hours between 10PM and 12AM are some of the most important hours a person can be asleep. It is very important that we reach what is called REM sleep so that we get what we need. We have already mentioned how important the immune system is with regards to chronic pain and dysfunction. This is the same case with sleep.

The Hoover Arthritis Research Center in Arizona reported "The central nervous system (CNS) modulates immune function by signaling target cells of the immune system through autonomic and neuroendocrine pathways. Neurotransmitter and hormones produced and released by these pathways interact with immune cells to alter immune functions, including cytokine production. Cytokines produced by cells of the immune and nervous systems regulate sleep" (Lorton et al, 2006). Statistics from the United States Centers for Disease Control and Prevention found that over 35 percent of Americans reported getting less than seven hours of sleep on average during a 24 hour period (Mercola, June 18 2011).

Glutathione is a very important matter. We have already mentioned this substance, but I think it is very important for the reader to know just how important it is. Low levels of glutathione wreak havoc in our bodies. Glutathione is often called the "master anti-oxidant." Glutathione protects our body from inflammation, free radicals, autoimmunity, and toxins. Dr. Mark Hyman, author of The UltraMind Solution, stated "glutathione is one of the single most important chemicals in the human body, and a deficiency in it can cause severe mental and physical health issues." Another recent study found that glutathione depletion is a common feature of neuropathic pain and diseases that involve the sensory neuron (Naziroglu et al, 2011). We often use glutathione when helping people with chronic pain. I use it myself and on my family on a regular basis. I think every person in America should use this supplement to some degree. Glutathione is a must for those people in chronic pain. Make sure that you use this substance in a transdermal manner. It is believed that this substance is not well absorbed in the stomach.

Inflammation often plays a very large role in chronic pain syndromes. We know that inflammation is our body's way of protecting us. In many acute health situations, inflammation is actually a good thing. Inflammation can actually protect us at times by providing cushioning against our environment. It is when inflammation becomes chronic that a problem arises. When an inflammatory situation does not go away, bad things happen. Inflammation is also the leading theory behind heart disease and cancer.

I really like ginger and tumeric for inflammation. Both of these substances have been used for hundreds of years for pain. The Journal of Pain had a study in 2010 that found that ginger was effective in helping muscle pain and inflammation. We routinely give ginger to our patients who are dealing with disc problems. Ginger also frequently helps people with digestion, which many people with chronic pain also have a problem with.

Inflammation is very important to look at. Chronic inflammation can stem from many things. So much of chronic inflammation comes from our lifestyle. Inflammation often comes from what we put into our bodies. Sugar, white flour and foods that we are allergic or reactive to are often the culprits. Sugar and white flour need to be minimized for everyone. We really need to limit our consumption of prepackaged foods. This is very important for those in pain. People with chronic health problems need proper testing to find what they are allergic or reactive to. We do not want to literally feed our pain.

Sugar can be a big problem. Researcher Malcolm Peet has also reported that too much sugar can actually cause harmful changes in your genes (Peet, 2004). It has been reported that the number one source of calories in the United States in from soda. Most of the chronic pain sufferers that come into my office are regular consumers of soft drinks. It has also been reported that more than 50% of Americans consume 180 pounds of sugar per year (Johnson & Gower, 2009). Eating too much sugar has been linked to: pain, anxiety, aggression, depression, eating disorders, fatigue, hyperactivity, and learning disorders.

Sugar replacements can cause an even bigger problem than sugar. I highly recommend that everyone in your family stay away from artificial sweeteners. As a general rule, if the substance was made in a lab, do not put it in your body. If a man made it in a lab, I am not sure we were meant to consume it. There are many reports of these artificial sweeteners being neurological poisons and cancer causing agents. Aspartame is believed to turn to formaldehyde in the body. Another one of these sweeteners is believed to turn into chlorine when it goes into a person's body. I do not know about you, but I really do not want chlorine or formaldehyde in my body.

Vitamin D is a very important subject when dealing with chronic pain. We look at the vitamin D levels of almost every patient we see, no matter what the chief complaint is. One study from the Mayo Clinic found that "all patients with persistent, nonspecific musculoskeletal pain are at high risk for the consequences of unrecognized and untreated severe hypovitaminosis D" (Plotnikoff & Quigley, 2003). That is a really important study. You need to let others know about it. The people that come in our office with chronic pain almost always have insufficient vitamin D levels. Many have very low levels of this extremely important vitamin. This is a perfect example of how deficient the average American diet is. Even the mainstream healthcare practitioners are catching on to the wonders of vitamin D.

A review on vitamin D supplementation trials, published in *The Archive of Internal Medicine*, reported a seven percent decrease in death from all causes with optimal levels of vitamin D (Hyman, 2009). This is unheard of for a supplement or vitamin. A seven percent decrease in death from all causes is a big deal. I make sure that everyone in my family gets vitamin D on a regular basis. Make sure everyone in your family routinely has their vitamin D levels checked. It is very rare to find a chronic pain patient who has optimal vitamin D levels.

Dr. Michael Holick has done a tremendous amount of research on Vitamin D. I highly recommend his book, The Vitamin D Solution. People need to really understand the importance of vitamin D in the body. Most of us are just not getting enough. Researchers from Harvard and the University of Colorado found that 70% of whites, 90% of hispanics, and 97% of blacks in America have insufficient blood levels of vitamin D (Holick, 2010). Vitamin D is a factor that just cannot be missed in the management of chronic pain. Another study found low vitamin D levels were associated with increased risk for cognitive impairment (Llewellyn, et al. 2010).

It is important to know if you are eating the right types of food for your particular body. Titus Lucretius Carus, a first century philosopher said, "What is food for some may be poison for other." Never has that been more true. Some of the foods people commonly eat can cause inflammatory or even autoimmune reactions in the body. Dr. Hyman has stated,

"Hidden food allergies are a major unrecognized epidemic in the twenty-first century." The only saving grace is that never has food reactivity laboratory testing been better. We are now able to find the root cause of many of these issues.

The main culprits people have problem with concerning foods are gluten, dairy, soy, yeast and eggs. Gluten is definitely the most common and most understood of the foods people are reactive to. Gluten is a part of wheat. Wheat is different today than it used to be. The proportion of gluten protein in wheat has increased enormously as a result of hybridization of wheat. It was reported that gluten disorder is four times more common today than it was in the 1950s (Rubio-Tapia, 2009).

The majority of healthcare providers still think an individual has to show an intestinal response to gluten to prove reactivity. This is wrong thinking. It has been reported in a psychiatry journal that patients with an enteropathy (disease of the the intestinal tract) represent only a third of patients with neurological manifestations and gluten sensitivity

(Pruss, 2007). Although I care if a patient has Celiac Disease, which is a type of gluten disease which involves enteropathy, I am really looking for gluten reactivity rather than trying to name a disease. Researchers have linked gluten sensitivity with myopathy or muscle pain and dysfunction (Muscle Nerve, 2007).

There are many disease processes that have been linked to gluten consumption in people that are gluten reactive. The conditions include: anxiety, depression, dementia, epilepsy, neuropathy, and schizophrenia. I have also seen gluten reactivity involved in chronic pain, adhd, autism and insomnia. One study linked headaches and CNS white matter abnormalities with gluten sensitivity (Hadjvassiliou et al., 2001). It amazes me how slow so many healthcare providers are to acknowledge the link between what a person eats and chronic health problems. It was not that long ago that testing for vitamin deficiencies was ridiculed. Now, blood testing for vitamin D deficiencies is a very common practice.

Our adult populations takes far too many drugs. Many

of these drugs contain toxic chemicals. I am not sure people would take all of the drugs they do if they truly knew what they were putting in their bodies. Some of these drugs contain things like aluminum, mercury, and even antifreeze. One of my favorite drugs to make fun of is the one made with pregnant horse urine. Who wants horse urine in their body? If people would only read the ingredients of what they put in their bodies they might make better choices.

Statin drugs in particular are causing a lot of problems. Many of these drugs lower CoQ10. CoQ10 has been shown to have positive effects on the heart, the immune system and energy levels. One recent study found that this substance protects our nervous system from oxidative stress (Won, Lee, and Lee; 2011). Another recent study found that a deficiency of CoQ10 was often found in patients who suffer from fibromyalgia (Cordero et al, 2010). Many of our chronic pain patients report a worsening of their symptoms after they start these cholesterol lowering drugs. I am not saying that there might not be those people who need drug intervention. I would strongly encourage everyone to keep their cholesterol down in a natural way if at all possible.

We know that acetaminophen lowers glutathione in the body. We also know that the number reason for liver failure in the United States on a yearly basis is acetaminophen (Tylenol). I recently saw an ad on a banner on a building promoting acetaminophen. The banner said poor posture causes headaches. Take our brand of acetaminophen for the headaches. The ad actually admitted the cause of the headaches and then suggested that you not fix the cause, just cover it up. That is one of the big problems of chronic health care issues. Many of the chronic pain sufferers have spent years covering up their symptoms instead of trying to determine the cause of their pain.

Many of the drugs people take for pain can cause huge problems. I am certainly not against using medications in a proper manner. I would gladly take the drugs in a life and death acute situation. I am against throwing more and more drugs at symptoms and hoping something good will happen.

This type of thinking has got to be stopped. Worse, many of the drug companies are committing all sorts of improper business practices including all sorts of fraud and deception. Unfortunately what is happening in healthcare today is very important to understand if people are to get better.

Pfizer, one of the world's largest drug companies, recently paid a 2.3 billion dollar fine for improper business practices. The fine interestingly enough was over its improper promotion of drugs commonly used to treat chronic pain. The world needs to wake up. Read what ingredients you are putting in your body. Read the history of the company that makes the drug. I am all for free enterprise and companies making profits, but when the health and future of the public is stake, we need better regulation.

There have been many more cases of abuse by the drug companies that people often trust. This is another example of how broken our system has become. The profits are so high for the drug industry that improper business acts have become the new way to do business. People are more important than profits. I think profits and win-win situations are a part of the United States. Profits at all costs are unacceptable. People are so used to the way things are done with chronic pain that they blindly accept junk treatment and go on their way without hope. The problem often begins with the healthcare providers though. More healthcare providers of all types need to keep up with the latest research without allowing the drug companies to distort the truth. Too many providers of all types rely far too heavily on the drug companies to tell them what is going on in research and patient care. I believe things can get better if healthcare providers start taking more time to really look at the literature with their own eyes.

Chapter 3:

The Symptoms

Chapter 3:

The Symptoms

"There is one thing stronger than all the armies of the world, and that is an idea whose time has come."

— Victor Hugo

T he time has come for healthcare providers to understand the cause of their patient's symptoms. Chronic pain sufferers can experience a wide variety of symptoms. The list can often be very long. Obviously, pain is a major issue. Pain that is almost always there. In some people the levels of pain change on a minute to minute basis, depending upon what they are doing, and in others the pain is a constant. Chronic pain is usually defined as having been present for more than three months in duration. It is amazing to see how different people with the same diagnosis present in my office. That is one reason it is so important not to completely buy into the labels. A diagnosis rarely tells the story of the individual and the individual's symptoms.

Most people deal with some form of anxiety and depression secondary to the pain they experience. I would say ninety percent of the people we help with chronic pain deal with some degree of anxiety and depression. Dealing with pain of a daily basis is enough to make anyone anxious or depressed. Worse, many of the medications add to the problem of anxiety and depression. We have seen more and more tardive dyskinesia lately. Tardive dyskinesia is the name for tremors that are caused by some of the antidepressants when taken for a period of time. Neurology also plays a big role in this as well. An over activated brainstem, the lower part of the brain, also adds to the anxiety issues. Calming down this area often helps people with anxiety feel better.

Many of the people dealing with chronic pain have gastrointestinal symptoms. Inflammation is almost always a problem in these cases. Most of these folks are not eating the proper foods for their body makeup/genetics. They are eating foods they are allergic or reactive to. I have found this scenario to be the case in over ninety percent of the chronic pain cases that come into our office. Some of these people have been diagnosed with Irritable Bowel Syndrome. This is an inflammatory disease process that usually results in severe abdominal pain and alternating severe constipation followed by explosive diarrhea.

Fatigue is a very common symptom associated with chronic pain syndromes. In fact, fibromyalgia is sometimes also called Chronic Fatigue Syndrome. I have never seen a patient with a chronic pain problem that did not have a significant amount of fatigue. The bottom line with fatigue is that it is almost impossible to have normal energy levels without proper fuel and activation for our body. People in pain rarely feel like exercising and a lack of exercise tends to make pain worse. It is a vicious cycle. I believe it also takes a tremendous amount of energy to deal with pain on a frequent basis.

Lets take some of the more common chronic pain syndromes and look at each in detail. I do not like labels nor do I care to place them on patients, but knowing what the labels mean can be important. Sometimes it is easier to understand what a person is dealing with if we know all of the components of an issue. Many people with these chronic pain diagnoses have never been informed of all of the aspects of their problem. I am constantly amazed at how little the average person with a chronic condition has been told about what they are dealing with.

Lets talk more about Fibromyalgia. A paper done by the UCLA School of Medicine called fibromyalgia "a mysterious pain syndrome with progressive and widespread pain, explicit areas of tender points, stiffness, sleep disturbance, fatigue, and psychological distress without any obvious disease" (Hsu, 2010). The Institute of Rheumatology in Israel calls fibromyalgia "a syndrome characterized by widespread pain and diffuse tenderness and is considered a multi-factorial disorder. Central nervous system sensitization is a major pathophysiological aspect of fibromyalgia, while various external stimuli such as infection, trauma and stress may contribute to the development of the syndrome" (Ablin, Neumann, and Buskila, 2008). Fibromyalgia is by far the most controversial of chronic pain syndromes or disorders. I call it the most controversial because most healthcare providers have a very poor understanding of what it is, let alone how to deal with it. That does not stop many of them from diagnosing it though. Some of the older healthcare providers still refuse to say that fibromyalgia is real. Some of the younger healthcare practitioners tell almost every chronic pain patient they see that the problem is fibromyalgia. If it were not such a serious situation it would almost be comical. I see the diagnosis of fibromyalgia often given to chronic pain patients when answers to the normal questions are hard to come by.

The word fibromyalgia is a mix of Latin and Greek that means pain of muscle and connective tissue. The Center for Disease Control and Prevention estimated in 2005 that five million adults in the United States were diagnosed with

Fibromyalgia. I believe that number has greatly increased since then. The bottom line symptoms are widespread pain and allodynia. Allodynia is a situation in which a person is very sensitive to pain at the slightest of stimuli. Most of the situations in which pain is felt is different than that of a normal person. That is perhaps why fibromyalgia is so misunderstood by friends and family members.

Often there are other symptoms with fibromyalgia such as: fatigue, sleep disorders, joint stiffness, bladder abnormalities, bowel abnormalities, numbness, tingling, memory problems, focus challenges, attention span difficulties and cognitive dysfunction. This cognitive dysfunction is often referred to as fibro fog. Fibromyalgia is thought to affect two to four percent of the population, with women receiving the diagnosis at a nine to one ratio. Fibromyalgia is also at times associated with people who have been diagnosed with Rheumatoid Arthritis and Lupus. The American College of Rheumatology uses the criteria for a clinical diagnosis of Fibromyalgia to include tenderness of at least eleven of eighteen specific spots with at least a three month duration. A paper published in Autoimmune Review in 2008 reported "Various triggers including trauma and stress as well as infections, may precipitate the development of FMS" (Buskin, Atzeni, Sarzi-Puttini, 2008).

Now lets talk about chronic disc problems. Disc problems will in many cases cause sciatica or severe leg/buttock pain. Very often disc problems are treated with epidural injections and surgery. There have been papers published that show epidural injections do not work well. According to the American Academy of Neurology's Therapeutics and Technology Assessment Subcommittee epidural steroid injections may only bring small, short-term relief (WebMD, 2007). The Academy of Neurology then went on to say that epidural steroid shots are not recommended for long-term back pain relief, improving back function or preventing back surgery.

There are not many people that are happy with the way their back surgeries have gone either. Rarely do these treatments provide lasting relief. In fact, the Foundation of Chiropractic Progress had a recent release which found that chiropractic adjustments prove equally beneficial as surgery in the treatment of sciatica. A recent report showed that laminectomies of the spine range from $50,000 - $150,000 and that spinal fusions range from $80,000 - $150,000. The bottom line is that a person should really avoid back surgery at almost any cost. We have an amazing treatment protocol that helps more than ninety percent of chronic disc patients achieve lasting relief. The process is called Intervertebral Disc Decompression or IDD for short.

Disc decompression is a very effective way to get the stress off of the disc and surrounding nerves and allow the area to heal. Disc decompression involves a gentle computerized pulling of the spine in an effort to take the stress off the problem area and promote healing and the exchange of nutrients. This is a painless procedure that many of the patients enjoy and some even fall asleep during the process. I fully believe that this procedure saved me from a lumbar disc surgery in 2009. I went from literally dragging around my right leg because of pain to being pain free in three weeks using this type of therapy on myself.

Here is a list of many of the diagnoses and symptoms we regularly see when dealing with chronic pain:

Arthritis- A catchall term that literally means joint inflammation used for the more than 100 forms of arthritis. The CDC reports that arthritis limits the activity of nearly twenty million adults in the United States. Fifty million adults, or one in five, have been diagnosed with this condition. Most commonly and for the information contained in this book is associated with the form called osteoarthritis. Osteoarthritis commonly affects the back, feet, hands, knees and hips. Many healthcare providers believe osteoarthritis can occur from altered biomechanics. Women are more affected than men. Symptoms of osteoarthritis joint pain, joint stiffness, aching around joints and tenderness on palpation. Risk factors include: trauma, obesity, sedentary lifestyle and poor biomechanics. One in two hundred and fifty children deal with some form of arthritis.

Back pain- Believe it or not another highly controversial issue in health care. Back pain results in more than $100 billion in U.S. healthcare costs each year, is always one of the leading causes of long-term disability and is one of the most frequently cited cause for both prescription and non-prescription medication. Chronic back pain almost always comes from a combination of altered biomechanics, muscle splinting, inflammation and poor inhibition of pain receptors. Usually the more chronic the back pain, the more the brain and lack of inhibition of pain receptors is involved. Back pain in its most severe forms can be as debilitating as almost any other chronic pain process.

Mainstream healthcare providers often miss the boat with back pain. Most of them just do not have enough training with back pain, the causes and the proper treatment. You just cannot throw drugs at back pain and hope it gets better. I see this far too much in practice. There are several papers regarding the lack of training in this area. A landmark study in Journal of Bone and Joint Surgery reported on a group of recent medical graduates. Eighty two percent of those students failed to demonstrate basic competency on a musculoskeletal competency exam. The authors of that study concluded, "We therefore believe that medical school preparation in musculoskeletal medicine is inadequate." The study was repeated four years later and the results were about the same. Their conclusions stated, "According to the standard suggested by the program directors of internal medicine residency departments, a large majority of the examinees once again failed to demonstrate basic competency in musculoskeletal medicine on the examination." Another example of this type of poor training was found by Matzkin et al in 2005 when they administered a standardized test of musculoskeletal competency to 334 medical students, residents and staff physicians. Their conclusion from the study stated, "Seventy-nine percent of the participants failed the basic musculoskeletal cognitive examination. This suggests that training in musculoskeletal medicine is inadequate in both medical school and non-orthopaedic residency training programs." These are issues most patients are just not aware of.

Stenosis- This disorder is basically a narrowing of the sac the spinal cord sits in. This can occur in the cervical, thoracic and lumbar spine. This is another problem that can many times be managed well with IDD therapy.

Lupus- a disease that is becoming more and more common. Systemic Lupus Erythematous (SLE) is an autoimmune condition the often affects the heart, joints, skin, lungs, blood vessels, the liver, kidneys and the nervous system. The initial complaints involving Lupus include: fever, fatigue, joint pain, and cognitive dysfunction. Later complaint involving Lupus often include: headache, depression, seizures, mood disorders, heart dysfunction, anxiety and skin disorders. With Lupus, a butterfly rash on the face is sometimes present.

Lupus or SLE occurs nine times more often in women than in men and is found very often between the ages of fifteen and thirty five. There are often periods of flare ups and remission. Lupus is often mistaken for other disorders and has been called the disease mimicker because it often mimics the symptoms of other disease processes. The normal course of treatment with this disorder is often corticosteroids and immunosuppressants.

Next, we will discuss TMJ dysfunction. We all have two temporo-mandibular joints. They are what many people think of as the jaw. In times of stress many people will start to grind and clench their teeth in either a wakeful or sleeping state. Often this happens in instances of increased stress or even pain. This pressure can cause dysfunction and improper gliding of the TMJ. Patients are often given night guards in an attempt to keep the compression and grinding from occurring.

Trigeminal Neuralgia is another chronic pain syndrome. Trigeminal Neuralgia is also know as tic douloureax. I have heard patients describe this disorder as a knife being repeatedly used to stab their face. Others have said it feels like electric shocks to the face. Regardless of the description, this disorder is thought to be one of the most painful to human beings. One in fifteen thousand people are diagnosed with Trigeminal Neuralgia with women over the age of fifty being the most predominant.

Rheumatoid Arthritis is something we are seeing more and more of lately. Unfortunately, the sufferers seem to be getting younger. We know that Rheumatoid Arthritis is an inflammatory autoimmune disorder in which the body is attacking its own joints in the cartilage. The hands, the feet and the cervical spine are most affected. The sufferer's joints usually become swollen, tender, warm, stiff and have limited range of motion. The incidence of Rheumatoid Arthritis is two to three times higher in women than in men with a peak incidence in the sixties.

Gout- This is a condition characterized by attacks of acute inflammatory arthritis. Most people think of the commonly occurring attacks on the big toe when they think of gout. This condition comes from elevated uric acid levels that lead to the inflammatory arthritis. Gout was talked about as far back as ancient Egypt.

Crohn's Disease- is an inflammatory disease of the intestines. The main symptoms include: abdominal pain, diarrhea, vomiting, weight loss, skin rashes, arthritis, infections of the eye, fatigue and poor concentration. Crohn's typical presentation occurs either in the teen and twenties or the fifties through seventies. The most common complication is blockage of the intestine due to swelling or scar tissue. This is one type of inflammatory bowel disease. Sores and ulcers are sometime found in the intestinal tract with this condition. Some sources believe Chron's is the result of an overactive Th1 cytokine response.

Ulcerative Colitis- This is a chronic gastrointestinal disorder that only involves the large bowel (the colon). This disorder is characterized by progressive loosening of the stool, bloody stools, skin lesions, joint pain, eye infections and liver disorders. Ulcerative Colitis generally is thought to have less complications than Crohn's Disease. Fifty percent of people with this condition have the mild version.

Complex Regional Pain Syndrome- Pain described as shooting and often severe. Is characterized by the severe pain, swelling, skin changes, increased sweating, softening/thinning of bones, joint tenderness/stiffness and restricted movement.

Restless Leg Syndrome- This is a neurological problem associated with the irresistible urge to moves one's leg, arm or torso. RLS may accompany other disorders such as Rheumatoid Arthritis, Peripheral Neuropathy and Fibromyalgia or stand alone by itself. Restless Leg Syndrome is often associated with injury or back surgery. The first description of this condition was in 1672 by the famous neuroscientist Sir Thomas Willis.

Peripheral Neuropathy is another chronic pain problem.

The symptoms of this disorder are usually pain, weakness, tingling and distal (toward the end of the arms or legs) numbness. This usually occurs due to damage of the nerves from certain disease processes or from the side effects of medication. This occurs frequently with diabetes and has even been linked to taking antibiotics. Dr. Jay Cohen, an associate professor of family and preventive medicine at the University of California, San Diego found the use of Cipro and other fluoroquinolone antibiotics had possible side effects "involving the peripheral nervous system such as tingling, numbness, burning pain, twitching, or spasms." Some of those cases written about in this study has symptoms that lasted longer than two years. People really need to know about the possible adverse affects of the drugs they are putting in their bodies. Peripheral neuropathy is a big problem. Approximately thirty million people in the United States deal with peripheral neuropathy A recent study looked at the relationship between statins, cholesterol lowering medications, and peripheral neuropathy. According to the research, the people who took statins were more likely to develop polyneuropathy, also known as peripheral neuropathy. Taking statins for one year raised the patient's risk by about fifteen percent. Those who took statins for two or more years, the additional risk rose to twenty six percent. By the way the study also found that those patients who were on statins had increased risk of heart failure, dizziness, cognitive impairment, cancer, pancreatic rot, and depression. (Mercola, January 2012). This is an especially interesting study to consider. I would strongly recommend that if you are considering taking a statin drug (especially chronic pain patients) that you look at all of the information and options out there. I am not totally against statin drug therapy. I just cannot ignore the facts. The British Medical journal reported in May 2010 that some doses and types of statins are linked with side effects such as liver and kidney problems and muscle weakness and cataracts.

Diabetic Neuropathy can also manifest as chronic pain. This problem is closely related to Peripheral Neuropathy. Diabetic Neuropathy is a disorder that usually describes pain/nerve disorder that occurs due to diabetes. Symptoms typically include: numbness, tingling, pain (often described as burning or electric), abnormal body sensations, diarrhea, erectile dysfunction, urinary incontinence, visual changes, dizziness, muscle weakness and muscle contractions (fasciculations).

Lyme Disease- This condition is from a tick-borne infectious disease. The early symptoms include: fever, headaches, fatigue, depression and a circular bulls-eye rash. Later symptoms include: joint dysfunction, heart dysfunction, and central nervous system dysfunction. This can be one of the most difficult conditions to help a patient with. Many healthcare providers will not accept patients with this diagnosis. These people can find some relief though.

Irritable Bowel Syndrome is a chronic pain problem I have had personal experience with. This disorder is usually characterized by extreme stomach pain/cramping with alternating bouts of constipation and diarrhea. Often, bloating is a problem. Inflammation and irritation of the bowels are thought to play a major role. At the age of twenty I was told by my healthcare provider that this condition was the result of my body aging. I knew that at twenty I certainly did not feel old and I knew a lot of older people who were not having the problems I was experiencing. At no time was my diet even considered. I was told to take Metamucil for the rest of my life and come in for anti-inflammatories when things got too bad. Through many of the treatments in this book I have not had any Irritable Bowel Syndrome symptoms in approximately sixteen years. I was told to expect to develop ulcerative colitis or Crohn's disease as I got older as the natural progression of Irritable Bowel Syndrome. Looking back on that time in my life, I realize how poorly trained that healthcare provider was. There was no testing done on me at all. I was given drugs based on my history.

Many of these chronic pain syndromes cross the lines of diagnosis. Many of the diagnoses are basically just an opinion. A study published by Georgetown University stated "CFS has significant overlap with systemic hyperalgesia (fibromyalgia), autonomic dysfunction (irritable bowel syndrome and migraine headaches), sensory hypersensitivity (dyspnea; congestion; rhinorrhea; and appreciation of visceral nociception in the esophagus, gastrointestinal tract, bladder, and other organs), and central nervous system maladaptations (central sensitization) recorded by functional magnetic resonance imaging (fMRI)" (Baraniuk and Zheng, 2010).

The time has come for people suffering with chronic pain to look for new ways to manage and possibly even defeat their conditions. Constantly taking drugs that will lower your body's immune response are not the only route with autoimmune conditions. Constantly taking drugs that will inhibit your pain receptors is not the only route with inflammatory conditions. Why not look for the cause? Remember, our environment, the functional state of our nervous system and what we put in our bodies often makes all the difference in the world.

Chapter 4:

Diagnosis/Labels/
Expectations

Chapter 4:

Diagnosis/Labels/Expectations

"Labels are only for cans."
— Dr. Andy Barlow

You or your love one are not labels. It is very important to not let the diagnosis you have received from a doctor, or even worse the self made diagnosis from the internet, define who you are. This happens far too much. Only the individual defines who they are. You are not your disease. You are not your condition. Many people who have dealt with chronic pain for a long time have difficulty believing there is any hope of management or relief of their pain. Calling a condition a certain name rarely helps defeat that condition. Many of the chronic pain syndromes are very close in nature. The

University of Michigan produced a study out of their Chronic Pain and Fatigue Research Center that found that "Many researchers have observed that Chronic Fatigue Syndrome shares features in common with other somatic syndromes, including irritable bowel syndrome, fibromyalgia, and temporomandibular joint dysfunction" (Clauw, 2010).

All too often the person is led to believe that all they can look forward to is adding two to three more drugs each year of their life. The average patient who is dealing with a chronic pain condition has seen twelve to fifteen other health care provider before seeing us. Many have gone to the famous hospital systems across the country and spent countless thousands of dollars and found no relief. That is very unfortunate and one of the major causes of so little hope among these people.

People are much more than the diagnosis they are given. Chronic pain sufferers really need to understand that point. Besides, many of the people we see are diagnosed incorrectly anyway. So many people come to us with the diagnosis of fibromyalgia when they do not even have that disorder.

Many of the diagnoses are based on opinion and history more than objective findings. Most doctors do not have the time or training to really search for the cause of the problem. Most people take their diagnosis of some form of chronic pain like they would a jail sentence. Know from here on out, there is hope for almost every single case.

That is one of the most common problems we have in helping people with chronic pain. Most people just believe that their health complaint is something they will have to suffer with for the rest of their life. Many of these folks are also dealing with brain dysfunction as well. Often the frontal lobe of the cerebral cortex is involved. Our frontal lobe contains a great deal of our personality and makes us who we are. Not only does a poorly functioning brain not deal with pain well but a poorly functioning brain does not make good decisions either. There are some cases that we recommend at least a consultation with some type of counselor. This is especially true in the chronic pain cases in which severe depression has come about.

Expectations are an enormous part of the equation. Most people with chronic pain really do not know what to expect from their condition. Most doctors do not have the time and very often the training to deal with these cases in an effective manner. Most people just recognize it as a bad situation. It is as if someone has put a weight around their neck. Saddling a person with this weight is never helpful. The person with the label and the families of that person suffer. There is a great book on managing expectations call <u>Leadership and Self-deception</u> by the Arbinger Institute. I highly recommend this book to people dealing with chronic situations.

I will admit that for a long time I thought the most important thing to do with a patient was to determine the correct diagnosis. That is often what all forms of healthcare providers are taught in school. Most of us had to learn these diagnoses for some type of national or state board. School and real life are two totally different arenas. I have learned that the most important thing to that patient is to feel better. Many do not care what you call their condition. Most of my patients cannot even remember the word mesencephalon. They care that you can help them. That is why the right type of examination is so important. That is why not giving in to a diagnosis is so important.

Another important point to get across is that managing and/or defeating chronic pain is a major undertaking. This process has to be a top priority. I often will tell people who are dealing with chronic pain that if the process of getting better is not in the top three in their list of priorities, this might not be the proper time to try. There is a big difference in finding out what is wrong and taking the proper steps in maximizing an individual's health. Besides time, this often also comes down to finances as well. Please do not think you will be able to rely on your insurance to have all of the testing and treatment done. Your health has to be more important than a copay. Some chronic pain cases are not that expensive and some are quite expensive. I highly encourage people to have all of the testing run on them and then decide if the care program is right for them at that time. You have to make all of this a major priority in your life or you will not get the results that you want.

Lets get to the touchy subject of finances. I will be quite frank with you when talking about finances with regard to testing and management of chronic pain. The bottom line is that your health must be more important than a copay. I cannot tell you how many times I have answered the question, "Why does my insurance not pay for this?" I will tell you like I tell them. I do not know. I constantly see insurance companies pay for drugs that people get addicted to and many that do not even work and yet will not pay for a service that works ninety percent of the time. Every year of practice I am amazed at how many people will choose surgical interventions that may not be necessary or even appropriate in their case based on what the insurance coverage is.

You must be willing to invest more in your health than a twenty dollar copay. Your health has to be more important than a copay. In today's insurance environment the bottom line for the insurance company is to make a profit.

An individual's health is not nearly as important to insurance companies as is the bottom line profit. I can assure you that a number cruncher sitting at a desk will not care what is the best test or therapy for you. Some of this testing can be expensive at times (between $500 and $2000 depending on many different variables ranging from mild to very severe).

With many of the people we work with we are able to get life changing, monumental results. A person cannot put a price on a life without drugs or a life with limited drug use and having no pain or a level of pain that is at least tolerable. Success to me in chronic pain cases is at least a fifty percent reduction in pain levels. We often do much better than a fifty percent reduction in pain. We are able to do this in at least ninety percent of the cases we accept. I will tell you that we only accept the cases we feel like a great deal of change is possible. There are some people who have passed the point of no return in chronic pain cases. We sometimes will take cases like this to help the person live a life that is at least a little more manageable.

The point of this chapter is that there is hope for sufferers of chronic pain. There are answers. These answers are often found in a non drug model of healthcare. I believe I have already made the case of how often these drugs are ineffective. I realize that approximately eighty percent of the people with any chronic health condition will never make the decision to see a healthcare provider like me. There are too many drug ads on television, radio and in print. There is no doubt who is David and who are the Goliaths. I can only help those people who are willing to take a chance. The reward is so worthwhile.

When talking about the case for hope in chronic pain cases I am reminded of one of my favorite metaphors in healthcare. It goes a little something like this. There is a fifty story building that you are in. You are on the fiftieth floor. You are the only one to know that there is a raging fire that cannot be stopped. You know you were meant for this task. You knock on every door on every floor of this building. You tell whoever opens it that there is a fire and you need to get out of the building. Many of the people cannot express their thanks enough. About two out of every ten doors tell you that you must be crazy. Prove to me that there is a fire. Now you have a decision to make at this point. Do you continue to knock on the doors and tell people about the raging fire or do you stand there and try to convince those people that the fire is real and the right thing to do is to get out of the building. I know the right answer for me. I would and do keep knocking on the next door. I know that I will never convince the nonbelievers, no matter how much proof I have.

Chapter 5:

The Normal Treatments

Chapter 5:

The Normal Treatments

"Most over the counter drugs and almost all prescribed drug treatments merely mask symptoms of health problems or in some way alter the way organs or systems such as the circulatory system work. Drugs almost never deal with the reasons why these problems exist, while they frequently create new health problems as side effects of their activities."

—John R. Lee, MD

The normal treatments for chronic pain almost always include trying to cover up the symptoms without ever finding the root or cause of the pain. The cause matters. Covering up one symptom almost always leads to trying to cover up more symptoms. How many chronic pain sufferers do you know that are on just one drug? If the drug worked so well, what are all of the other drugs for? The average senior over the age of sixty five is on an estimated more than thirty one prescriptions! Healthcare providers can do better than that. The bottom line point is that acute protocols rarely work in chronic situations.

Our healthcare system is a broken system. Most traditional healthcare providers are too busy to stay up on the current research and rely far too much on the drug companies for their latest information. The drug company's bottom line is profit. Doctors should be very careful who they get their information from. There is far too many drugs being used for purposes other than which they were approved. Most people suffering with chronic pain blindly trust these doctors that give them the latest drug without understanding the side effects. I do not believe doctors of any kind should rely solely on the drug companies for answers. You have got to figure out if your healthcare provider is one who stays up to date on the current literature out there. If they are not, try another provider.

The two most common drugs that we see chronic pain

sufferers on are Lyrica and Cymbalta. I believe these two drugs are far to overprescribed. We also often see these people on anti-seizure drugs (neurontin/gabapentin), anti-depressant drugs, muscle relaxers, pain killers, and opioids. Like we said before, many of these drugs have the potential to be quite dangerous to the person taking them.

Opioids are commonly used for chronic pain despite a lack of clinical trials. Investigators at the European League Against Rheumatism announced in 2009 that an analysis of fifty two thousand fibromyalgia patients found that forty percent received an opioid. Addiction is a major problem in the chronic pain syndrome population. It is simply amazing at the number of people who rely on this type of drug for their every day functioning.

The following is a list of some of the most routinely given drugs in the treatment of chronic pain. This is by no means a complete list. These are the drugs patients who come see us are routinely on. I would bet that most people taking these drugs do not know the back story or the full list of side effects of these drugs. Get ready. Much of the information found for this list was found at Drugs.com.

Lyrica- Is the first drug approved for use in people with fibromyalgia. Lyrica was first used as a anti seizure medication. The Wall Street Journal reported in 2009 that Lyrica was one of the drugs involved in fabricated data used in research studies. In the largest health care fraud settlement in history, the drug maker of Lyrica was fined $2.3 billion to resolve allegations that the company illegally promoted uses of four of its drugs, including Lyrica. It has been reported that this drug "increases the risks of suicidal thoughts and behaviors, lose your memory and your hair" (Mercola, 2010). Its many possible side effects include: hives, difficulty breathing, swelling of face/lips/tongue/throat, mood changes, behavior changes, depression, anxiety, insomnia, agitation, hostility, restlessness, hyperactivity, suicidal thoughts, muscle pain, weakness, tenderness, easy bruising/bleeding, swelling, weight gain, dizziness, drowsiness, anxiety, loss of balance or coordination, problems with memory or concentration, dry mouth, skin rash or itching, constipation, stomach pain, increased appetite, and joint pain (Drugs.com). This drug is constantly advertised on television for chronic pain.

Topomax- Another anti-seizure medication. Possible side effects include: difficulty breathing, mood changes, anxiety, panic attacks, trouble sleeping, feeling impulsive, irritable, agitated, hostile, aggressive, restless, hyperactive, more depressed, thoughts of suicide or hurting yourself, sudden vision loss, pain around or behind your eyes, dry mouth, increased thirst, drowsiness, decreased sweating, increased body temperature, hot/dry skin, slowed thinking, memory problems, trouble concentrating, speech problems, balance problems, confusion, mood changes, unusual behavior, vomiting, loss of appetite, tired feeling, irregular heartbeats, feeling like you might pass out, severe pain in your side of lower back, painful or difficult urination, numbness, tingly feeling, diarrhea, weight loss, feeling nervous, change in your sense of taste, and cold symptoms such as stuffy nose, sneezing and sore throat.

Lamictal- Yet another anti-seizure medication. Possible side effects include: severe or life-threatening skin rash, thoughts about suicide, mood/behavior changes, depression, anxiety, feeling agitated, hostile, restless, hyperactive, tremors, headache, fever, chills, neck stiffness, increased sensitivity, confusion, nausea, vomiting, chest pain, body aches, flu symptoms, easy bruising, unusual bleeding (nose, mouth, vagina or rectum), purple or red pinpoint spots under your skin, dizziness, drowsiness, blurred vision stomach pain, upset stomach, loss of coordination, back pain, weight loss, menstrual pain, sleep problems, runny nose, and sore throat (Drugs.com).

Cymbalta- An antidepressant. A serotonin and norepinephrine re-uptake inhibitor. Possible side effect include: mood or behavior changes, anxiety, panic attacks, trouble sleeping, feeling impulsive, irritable agitated, hostile, aggressive.

restless. hyperactive. more depressed, thoughts of suicide, nausea, stomach pain, itching, loss of appetite, dark urine, clay-colored stools, jaundice (yellowing of the skin or eyes), feeling like you might pass out, agitation, hallucinations, fever, fast heart rate, overactive reflexes, very stiff muscles, high fever, sweating, confusion , fast or uneven heartbeats, tremors, easy bruising, unusual bleeding painful or diffi-cult urination, headaches, trouble concentrating, memory problems, weakness, feeling unsteady, loss of coordination, fainting, seizure, shallow breathing or breathing that stops, dry mouth, drowsiness, tired feeling, mild nausea or loss of appetite, and constipation (Drugs.com). Another drug that is hard to not see the television commercials for.

Neurontin- Another anti-seizure medication. Often used to treat nerve pain caused by herpes or shingles. The same com-pany that makes this drug makes Lyrica. The drug maker paid $430 million for illegally promoting uses (Mercola, 2011). Possible side effects include: thoughts of suicide, mood/

behavior change, depression, anxiety, feeling agitated, hostile, restless, hyperactive, increased seizures, fever, chills, body aches, flu symptoms, swelling of your ankles or feet, confusion, rapid back and forth movement of your eyes, tremor, easy bruising, memory problems, trouble concentrating, acting restless, acting hostile, acting aggressive, dizziness, drowsiness, weakness, feeling tired, lack of coordination, blurred vision, nausea, vomiting, stomach pain, loss of appetite, diarrhea, constipation, runny or stuffy nose, sore throat, headache, insomnia, unusual dreams, acne, and mild skin rash (Drugs.com).

Vicodin- A combination of acetaminophen and hydrocodone. It is in a group of drugs called narcotic pain relievers. Possible side effects include: impairment of thinking or reactions, shallow breathing, slow heartbeat, feeling light-headed, fainting, confusion, fear, unusual thoughts or behavior, seizures (convulsions), problems with urination, nausea, upper stomach pain, itching, loss of appetite, dark urine, clay-colored stools, jaundice (yellowing of the skin or eyes), feeling anxious, dizzy, or drowsy, mild nausea, vomiting, upset stomach, constipation, headache, mood changes, blurred vision, ringing in our ears, and dry mouth.

Celebrex- According to a 2005 study, those people taking 200 mg of this drug twice per day more than doubled their risk of dying of cardiovascular disease (Mercola, 2006). Those people on 400 mg twice per day more than tripled their risk.

Soma- Possible side effects include: constipation, diarrhea, dizziness, drowsiness, headache, indigestion, lightheadedness, nausea, stomach pain, vomiting, black/tarry/bloody stools, blurred vision, fainting, fast heartbeat, fever, chills, persistent sore throat, loss of coordination, agitation, depression, irritability, ringing in the ears, seizures, severe or persistent trouble sleeping, shallow or very slow breathing, tremors, unusual bruising or bleeding, vomit that looks like coffee grounds and wheezing.

Loritab- Possible side effects include: drowsiness, mental clouding, lethargy, impairment of mental and physical performance, anxiety, fear, dysphoria, psychic dependence, mood changes, constipation, urinary retention, hearing impairment, skin rash, itching, and cramps. This seems to be the drug of choice in the earlier phases of normal care for chronic pain patients.

Percoset- Possible side effect include: constipation, dizziness, drowsiness, flushing, lightheadedness, mental/mood changes, nausea, vision changes, vomiting, respiratory depression, apnea, respiratory arrest, circulatory depression, hypotension, shock, skin eruptions, heart dysrhythmias, palpitations, dehydration, elevations of hepatic enzymes, hepatic failure, jaundice, hearing loss, tinnitus, asthma, visual disturbances, drug abuse, depressed level of consciousness, hallucination, depression and suicide.

Tramadol- Possible side effects include: agitation, hallucinations, fever, fast heart rate, overactive reflexes, nausea, vomiting, diarrhea, loss of coordination, fainting, seizures, blistering red rash, shallow breathing, weak pulse, dizziness, spinning sensation, constipation, upset stomach, drowsiness, feeling nervous or anxious.

Oxycontin- Possible side effects include: shallow breathing, slow heartbeat, seizure, cold/clammy skin, confusion, severe weakness, dizziness, feeling light-headed, fainting, nausea, vomiting, constipation, loss of appetite, headache, feeling tired, dry mouth, sweating, and itching.

Effexor- Possible side effects include: seizures, very stiff (rigid) muscles, high fever, sweating, confusion, fast or uneven heartbeats, tremors, feeling like you might pass out, agitation, hallucinations, overactive reflexes, nausea, vomiting, diarrhea, loss of coordination, headache, trouble concentrating, memory problems, weakness, feeling unsteady, confusion, fainting, shallow breathing, breathing that stops, cough, chest tightness, trouble breathing, easy bruising, drowsiness, dizziness, feeling nervous, strange dreams, increased sweating, blurred vision, dry mouth, changes in appetite or weight, mild nausea, constipation, decreased sex drive, and impotence.

Morphine- This drug is thankfully used for many people at the end of their lives to help manage uncontrollable pain. This drug can be very addictive and can cause many problems to people in non end of life situations.

Acetaminophen- This is a drug that I mistakenly believed was very safe. This drug is the number one cause of liver failure in the United States on a yearly basis. There are actually trial lawyers that call themselves acetaminophen lawyers because of the number of problems with this drug. A lot of people think that because a drug is available over the counter that it is safe. You still have to be very careful. Possible side effects include: low fever with nausea, stomach pain, loss of appetite, dark urine, clay-colored stools, jaundice (yellowing of the skin or eyes), and liver problems. We have seen patients taking this drug regularly for only one to two weeks that have liver problems. In May of 2011, Reuters reported that chronic acetaminophen users had nearly twice the risk of developing cancer (Reuters May 9, 2011). It was also found by the Fred Hutchinson Cancer Research Center in Seattle that 9 percent of the study participants who used large amounts of acetaminophen developed blood cancer (Mercola, May 25 2011).

Ibuprofen- Another drug that most people think is harmless. Possible side effects include: chest pain, weakness, shortness of breath, slurred speech, problems with vision or balance, black, bloody, or tarry stools, coughing up blood or vomit that looks like coffee grounds, swelling, rapid weight gain, urinating less than usual or not at all, nausea, stomach pain, low fever, loss of appetite, dark urine, clay-colored stools, jaundice (yellowing of the skin or eyes), fever, sore throat, headache, severe blistering, peeling, red skin rash, bruising, severe tingling, numbness, pain, muscle weakness, neck stiffness, chills, increased sensitivity to light, seizures, upset stomach, mild heartburn, diarrhea, constipation, bloating, gas, dizziness, nervousness, skin itching, rash, blurred vision, and ringing in the ears (Drugs.com).

Naproxen- Possible side effects include: chest pain, weakness, shortness of breath, slurred speech, problems with vision or balance, black, bloody or tarry stools, coughing up blood or vomit that looks like coffee grounds, swelling or rapid weight gain, urinating less than usual or not at all, nausea, stomach pain, low fever, loss of appetite, dark urine, clay-colored stools, jaundice (yellowing of the skin or eyes), fever, sore throat, headache with severe blistering, peeling, red skin rash, bruising, severe tingling, numbness, pain, muscle weakness, neck stiffness, chills, increased sensitivity to light, purple spot on the skin, upset stomach, mild heartburn or stomach pain, diarrhea, constipation, bloating, gas, dizziness, nervousness, skin itching, rash, blurred vision and ringing in the ears.

Aspirin- So many people think this is a harmless substance. I grew up thinking aspirin was no big deal. Possible side effects include: black, bloody or tarry stools, coughing up blood or vomit that looks like coffee grounds, severe nausea, vomiting, stomach pain, swelling, hearing problems, ringing in the ears, upset stomach, heartburn, drowsiness, and heartburn.

Vioxx- A drug that was thankfully taken off the market due to all of the problems. I list this drug because I believe it resembles some of the other drugs currently being used. As many people that this drug harmed and as many lawsuits that were paid off, this drug still made the manufacturer money. No wonder things with the drug industry have gotten so out of hand.

Drugs are very rarely the long term answer to any questions. Our country really cannot afford to continue on this route. The United States is expected to spend greater than one trillion dollars on drugs by 2013 (Mercola, 2008). We have more drugs in our country than any other country in the world. If the drugs work, why does America consistently rank among the lowest of the industrialized nations on the health scores of our people. The drugs fail over and over for chronic conditions.

The bottom line here is that the drug companies have far too much power and influence in the healthcare industry and in every day life. You cannot watch television or listen to the radio without being told to ask your doctor if a specific drug is right for you. Doctors have become far too dependent on the drug reps for their current information.

The drug industry is consistently one of the top lobbying groups in Washington. As great as our country has been in the past, I am concerned with how we have let big business gain so much power. I believe we live in the greatest country in the world and we can take back that power if we are properly informed and make the right choices. I am glad that the drug companies are there if we need them, but we have let them become far too powerful and far too able to manipulate the patient and the doctor. The time for change has arrived. The consumers have the power to put the drug companies back in their proper place.

I very much appreciate the quote of columnist Martha Rosenberg, who said, " In the pharmaceutical industry's rush to get drugs to market, safety usually comes last. Long studies to truly assess a drug's risks just delay profits after all—and if problems do emerge after medication hits the market settlements are usually less than profits. Remember, Vioxx still made money."

Chapter 6:

What Makes Our Treatment Different

Chapter 6:

What Makes Our Treatment Different

"You will observe with concern how long a useful truth may be known and exist, before it is received and practiced upon."

— Benjamin Franklin

The most exciting part about our treatment plan is that we have brought together the most effective treatments together under one roof. I believe we have one of the most contemporary programs for helping people with chronic pain syndromes in the country. I am always on the lookout for new ways to help people with chronic pain, autoimmune problems, and so called helpless situations. The answers seem to always, in some form or another, involve the brain. Research is coming out at a very fast rate in this segment of healthcare. We are living in very exciting times when it comes to being able to help people in pain. My hope is that besides people with chronic pain, others will read this book. Too many doctors in mainstream medicine are locked into only what their peers are doing. What if their peers offer a low level of service?

Another important aspect of my care plan is that each person is seen as an individual. This is a key factor. It amazes me that some providers see that as success with a patient. Healthcare has become too obsessed with naming the dysfunction or disease. Waiting until a person is sick enough to receive an insurance code is wrong. Individuals are much more than insurance codes. Insurance has really messed up the way healthcare is practiced.

Each person we help is just a little bit different. Those differences are important to recognize. Recognizing these differences can make all the difference. Many of the people we see are given real answers for the first time. Many finally feel some type of validation because their former healthcare provider just did not believe them. Most of the healthcare providers that do not believe their patients do not even understand the nature of the problem.

We have incorporated the use of neurofeedback in our chronic pain program to help diminish the pain that the person suffers from. I strongly believe that this technology is on the brink of really taking off across all of the disciplines of healthcare. We said earlier that this type of treatment involves training the brain with EEG leads and a computer while the individual watches a movie or listens to music. Neurofeedback has been studied for many years. This form of care for the nervous system is very important. I find it hard to believe it has taken so long for this to become mainstream. During the 1960s, NASA studied the process and its effects on brain (Demos, 2004).

The vast majority of our patients like neurofeedback. I have found it very helpful for myself and my family as well. Not only do we see chronic pain diminish, but many patients report having less anxiety and depression and that they sleep better. It is almost like a workout for the brain. We are able to train the brain what its proper brain wave make up is based on brain mapping. Brain mapping involves the patient wearing a cap fitted with electrodes that measure brain waves. The readings are then compared against a normative database and the report is made.

We also are using the most advanced nutritional supplementation available and we are able to monitor and make sure the nutrients are working with laboratory testing. This is not a faith based program. A person gets to see lab work that backs up the diagnosis and the treatment protocol. We often use glutathione, nitric oxide, and vitamin D with our chronic pain patients. These three supplements are incredibly powerful when used in the correct manner and are backed up by many studies.

We use the laboratory numbers used by functional medicine instead of the normal disease state numbers that are used by the majority of healthcare providers. I care how a person is responding and feeling. I also care about the numbers. It is important to get an objective feedback on how much we are helping a person.

Checking numbers for cortisol, vitamin D, food reactivity, and other metabolic factors is so important. I am a big fan of supplements and good nutrition. Proper testing really shows the importance of using the correct form of supplements and nutrition. Checks and balances in any system are very important. Having objective measurements are very important with chronic pain cases.

One of the things I am most proud about our system of management for chronic pain is the fact that we turn over every rock to see what the cause is. This is so important in the understanding and the management of chronic pain. This is something that more sufferers of chronic pain must demand from their healthcare providers. Do not just accept what an insurance company will pay for. I love to hear other healthcare providers make comments about how many variables we look at in a number of cases.

My management program for all types of chronic pain

works. We get results. The results are tangible. Patients are literally able to see their lives change for the better right in front of them. That is the most important part. Our patients also do not experience the side effects that are associated with many of the drug therapies. I cannot hold a candle to the budget of the drug companies, but I can tell you that what we do has never hurt anyone. The drug companies cannot say that. Dr. Mercola recently reported that only six percent of drug advertising material is supported by scientific evidence. So the majority of what you hear in a drug commercial may or may not be true.

The things we do for chronic pain will not make you want to commit suicide, have depression or anxiety or make you bleed from different parts of your body. My plan will not make a person a drug addict or make them vomit something up that looks like coffee grounds. My plan changes an individual's life, as well as their family. It is too easy to see if someone is a good candidate for my pain management program. Give us an hour to two hours of your time to find out if this is right for you and your specific case.

Chapter 7:

What It Takes

Chapter 7:

What It Takes

"Action may not always bring happiness, but there is no happiness without action."

— Benjamin Disraeli

To defeat and or manage chronic pain requires great effort. In many cases, it requires individuals and families to change very large portions of their lives. The sacrifices can be tough. The rewards are great. I have never had anyone reach their healthcare goals and say it was not worth it, however. A life without pain and without long term use of dangerous drugs is a great thing. I have seen many lives literally change before my eyes when people get out of pain. It has been such a honor over the years to help people reach their health goals without the use of drugs or surgery.

It is important for everyone closely involved with the person who has chronic pain to understand the causes and process of healing. We have found that to make a profound difference. Chronic pain is rarely just in the person's head as they are often told by doctors who are not sure what they are dealing with. Many people with chronic pain deal not only with their pain, but with family members and friends doubting that their pain is real. That case always reminds me of a professor that used to tell our class in college that almost everyone is down on what they are not up on. Most people who have not experienced chronic pain for themselves rarely understand what that individual is dealing with. If you have dealt with that situation, I am here to tell you that there is hope for you.

If you are ready to get better, let me give you some advice. These are my recommendations for you to have success in managing chronic pain. Management, and in many cases, recovery, is possible. This is a results driven program. I am always amazed at the amount of healthcare practitioners who claim to use only properly referenced peer reviewed treatments. In many cases of chronic pain, the mainstream way to deal with chronic pain is not supported by anything other than drug companies. I think many of them are too busy to read the current literature. Managing chronic pain without drugs is very possible.

First, you should get your brain mapped. This is such an exciting tool to have. This is like having a blueprint of the individual brain. It is important to find out how great the functional neurological component is. We have to know what is going on in the frontal lobe and motor/sensory strip of the brain. We have to know how the electrical component of the brain is working if we are to reach our goals. A person may never reach their optimal potential without this portion of the care program. The test also determines how strong of a candidate a person is for this type of recovery program.

Next, you should have a specific functional neurological evaluation to determine if functional disconnection syndrome is a part of the problem. I cannot stress enough how important this is. This is where the training your doctor has received is so important. It is very important to know how the cortex of the brain is communicating between the two hemispheres and with the rest of the body. It is very important for your doctor to realize that drugging the nervous system rarely makes any long term change. This checkup is as vital as the brain mapping in making sure how successful a recovery program will be.

Next, you have to get the food reactivity testing done. This is very important. This helps identify if you are properly fueling or poisoning your body. It is imperative to know if you are properly fueling your brain and nervous system. This is overlooked so often by healthcare providers who try to help people with chronic pain. There are many documented cases of gluten reactivity mimicking very serious neurological disorders. Look this stuff up for yourself. The research is out there. One of the best places to look is www.pubmed.gov. If you have the time, you really need to become an expert of your dysfunction. I wanted to overlook this portion of chronic pain for a long time. The literature was just too overwhelming to ignore.

Beyond the food reactivity testing, you must be committed to giving up processed foods. We know the average American eats close to their body weight in sugar on a yearly basis (Johnson & Gower, 2009). We need to limit the amount of toxins in our body, especially the food that we consume. We know that the average American consumes approximately one gallon of pesticide each year (Hyman, 2009). Many people,especially family members, will have opinions about the food. The vast majority of them are wrong.

It is very important to have your body's cortisol burden checked. It must be checked in a very specific way several times throughout the day. Not only do the levels need to be considered, but also the overall rhythm as well. Remember, cortisol is not a bad thing. Cortisol was designed to regulate your glucose levels. Different types of stress can cause the adrenal glands to release abnormal amounts of cortisol. You have to know if there is adrenal dysfunction. Chronic cortisol problems can cause many health issues, including chronic pain. Cortisol can literally poison your brain if left unchecked.

Next on the list is vitamin D. Everyone should have their vitamin D levels checked on a yearly basis, even children. Dr. Michael Holick has done some incredible research on the subject of vitamin D. I strongly encourage you to read <u>The Vitamin D Solution</u> by Dr. Holick. This is especially important for chronic pain sufferers. Vitamin D is something I make sure my family takes on a regular basis.

Inflammation is another huge factor. I think I could write a book on just this alone. The future of healthcare really involves the modulation of inflammation. Chronic inflammation destroys the brain and nervous system. Chronic inflammation can cause pain and dysfunction everywhere in the body. Chronic inflammation can come from a wide variety of factors. Inflammation is often overlooked in traditional healthcare. There are many good ways to reduce inflammation that do not have side effects.

Learn to find ways to get ginger and turmeric into your diets. You should try and learn to cook with these spices if you can. They are so powerful in the fight against chronic inflammation. If you cannot, it is a great idea to use a supplement with one or both of these ingredients. Our disc patients often take 500 mg of ginger on a daily basis to help with inflammation in the musculoskeletal system.

You have to get some form of exercise. This is not a choice. You must do it. You cannot use pain as an excuse to not get exercise. Here is some very good news. Walking counts. If you are unable to walk, upper body ergometers are a great choice. We often use upper body ergometers in the office when we are helping people with chronic pain syndromes. Upper body ergometers look like a bicycle for your hands. Everyone out there needs some form of exercise on a daily basis for at least twenty to thirty minutes. It is ok to break the times up into more manageable units if needed.

Autoimmune testing can be very helpful with chronic pain issues. Many of our patients with chronic pain syndromes have autoimmune thyroid disease that had not been previously found. The name for autoimmune thyroid disease is Hashimoto's disease. Blood testing can be very helpful in determining if there is or is not an autoimmune component. Knowing this information is worth its weight in gold as far as getting results.

There will likely be some difficult food choices to make. Beyond reactivity testing, a person must be willing to give up processed foods and fast foods. Fast and cheap food almost never add up to nutritious and worthwhile food. Food planning can help you make better decisions. Going to the grocery store hungry and without a plan almost never turns out well. That is major reason the younger a patient with chronic pain is the more help they will require from people close to them at the beginning of a care program. Older people seem to be more open to changing the way they will eat if it will help in the long run.

Learn to like water. I hope you already are drinking water. The majority of our body is made up of water. It really is important that you are drinking at least six glasses of water per day. Make sure you are not consuming drinks with artificial sweeteners in them. These artificial sweeteners break down into neurotoxins in the body. Make sure you are drinking clean water. There have been some very nice products brought to market lately that have just enough real fruit flavor to make a difference. They contain no added sweeteners. Try them out.

Be committed to giving up soft drinks as well. The bottom line is that they are just not good for our bodies. You can get used to just about anything if the end justifies the means. Feeling better is much more important than a soda. Please do not think that a diet soda is any better for you.

You must be checked for vertebral subluxation. Most people have never even heard of vertebral subluxation. This a situation in which the bones of the spinal column become misaligned or fixated and cause stress to the nervous system. We have to know there are usually no glaring biomechanical problems in any type of chronic pain syndrome. We know that stress to the nervous system is almost always involved with chronic pain.

It is very important for all of us to be on some type of omega-3 fat supplementation. Omega-3 helps the brain, the overall nervous system and deals with inflammation. I feel very strongly about omega-3 supplementation. Fats are very important in the production of our hormones, which often play a huge role in chronic pain.

Last, but certainly not least, you must have hope. People that have hope get better faster. People that have a reason to get better, get better faster. You do not have to believe you will get better to get results in the program I have gone over. This is not a faith based healthcare program, but it makes for a better partnership if you do.

If I can help you in any way, please feel free to email my office. Our office website is DrJeremyMartin.com. There is hope for you. We help people all over the United States as well as all over the world. If we are unable to see you personally, we are often able to lead you in the direction of a healthcare provider trained in a similar manner.

Here is a quote I like to use with chronic pain patients as well as myself:

Through adversity we find strength;

Through sickness we recognize the value of health;

Through evil, the value of good;

Through hunger, the value of food;

Through exertion, the value of rest.

-Greek saying

I hope this book has helped bring hope to those in chronic pain. This book was written with those people in mind. I hope that it has opened some minds to those who know people in chronic pain. I hope that it has made at least a few healthcare providers examine what they thought they knew about chronic pain.

References

Ablin, Neumann, Buskila, 2008. Pathogenesis of fibromyalgia-a review. Joint Bone Spine. 2008 May; 75 (3):273-9.

Alsheikh-Ali, AA, Karas, RH, 2010. Balancing the intedned and unintended effetw of statins. British Medical Journal. 2010. May 20; 340: c2240.doi:101136/bmj.c2240.

American Pain Society (2012). Chronic Pain in America: Roadblocks to Relief. Retrieved January 18, 2012, from http://ampainsoc.org/resources/roadblocks/conclude_road.htm

Arnett, SV; Alleva, LM; Korossy-Horwood, R; Clark, IA; 2011. Chronic fatigue syndrome-a neurological model. Medical Hypothesis, 2011 Jul; 77 (1): 77-83. Epub 2011 Apr 6.

Baio et al, 2008. Autoimmune diseases and infections: controversial issues. Clinical and Experimental Rheumatology. 2008 Jan-Feb; 26 (1 Suppl 48): S74-80.

Baraniuk, JN, Zheng, Y, 2010. Relatoinships among rhinitis, fibromyalgia, an chronic fatigue. Allergy Asthma Proceedings. 2010 May-June; 31 (3): 169-78.

Beck, R. (2008). *Functional Neurology for Practitioners of Manual Therapy*. Philadelphia: Elsevier Health.

Bellanti et al, 2005. Are attention deficit hyperactivity disorder and chronic fatigue syndrom allergy related? What is fibromyalgia? Allergy and asthma proceedings: the official journal of regional and state allergy societies. 2005 Jan-Feb; 26 (1): 19-28.

Black, CD; Herring, MP; Hurley, DJ; O'Connor, PJ, 2010. Ginger (Zingiber officinale) reduces muscle pain caused by eccentric exercise. 2010 Sep; 11 (9): 894-903.

Buffalo News (2011). Chronic pain becomes common child complaint. Retrieved January 18, 2012, from http://www.buffalonews.com/life/health-parenting/health/article 687038.ece

Buskila, D, Atzeni, F, Sarzi-Puttini, P, 2008. Etiology of fibromyalgia: the possible role of infection and vaccination. Autoimmune Review. Oct; 8 (1): 41-3.

Clauw, 2010. Perspectives on fatigue from the study of chronic fatigue syndrome and related conditions. PM&R: the journal of injury, function, and rehabilitation. 2010 May: 2 (5): 414-30.

Cordero. 2010. Neuro Endocrinology Letters. Oxidative stress and mitochondrial dysfunction in fibromyalgia.

Costhelper (2010, January). Back Surgery Cost. Retrieved June 22, 2011, from http://www.ampainsoc.org/resources/roadblocks/conclude_road.htm

Demos, J. (2004). *Getting Started With Neurofeedback*. New York: W.W. Norton & Company.

Evans, J.(2009). *Handbook of Neurofeedback*. New York: Informa Healthcare.

Freedman, KB, Bernstein, J, 2002. Educational deficiencies in musculoskeletal medicine. The Journal of bone and joint surgery. American volume. 2002 Apr; 84-A(4): 604-8.

Hadjvassiliou et al, 2007. Myopathy associated with gluten sensitivity. Muscle & Nerve Journal, 35 (4): 443-450.

Hadjvassiliou, M; Grunewald, RA; Davies-Jones, GAB, 2001. Gluten sensitivity as a neurological illness. Journal of Neurology Neurosurgery and Psychiatry, 72: 560-563.

Holick, M.(2010). *The Vitamin D Solution*. New York: Penguin Group.

Hsu. 2010. American Journal of Therapeutics. 2011 Nov: 18(6): 487-509. Acute and chronic management in fibromyalgia: updates on pharmacotherapy.

Johnson and Gower (2009). *The Sugar Fix*. New York: Scribner.

Kharrazian, D. (2010). *Why Do I Still Have Thyroid Symptoms? When My Labe Tests Are Normal: A Revolutionary Breakthrough In Understanding Hashimoto's Disease and Hyperthyroidism.* Hampton: Morgan James Publishing.

Lorton et al, 2006. Bidirectional communication between the brain and immune system: implications for physiolobical sleep and disorders with disrupted sleep. Neuro-immunomodulation, 2006; 13 (5-6): 357-74.

Llewellyn, et al, 2010. Vitamin D and Risk of Cognitive Decline in Elderly Persons. Archives of Internal Medicine. 170 (13): 1135-1141.

Matzkin, E, Smith, EL, Freccero, D, Richardson, AB, 2005. Adequacy of education in musculoskeletal medicine. Journal of bone and joint surgery. American Edition. 2005 Feb; 87(2): 310-4.

Mercola. (2012, January 25). Nerve Damage With Cholesterol Meds. Retrieved February 9, 2012, from http://articles.mercola.com/sites/articles/archive/2012/01/25/nerve-damage-with-cholesterol-meds.aspx

Mercola. (2011, December 15). Taking Just a Little Too Much Tyleno Can Be Deadly. Retrieved January 30, 2012, from http://articles.mercola.com/sites/articles/archive/2011/12/15/little-too-much-tylenol-can-be-deadly.aspx

Mercola. (2011, November, 24). The #1 Cause of Accidental Death in the US- Are You At Risk? Retrieved January 18, 2012, from http://artibles.mercola.com/sites/articles/archive/2011/11/24/modern-medicine-disease-treatments.aspx

Mercola. (2011, July, 2). New Research Finds Doctors are Massively Overprescribing Drugs. Retrieved January 18, 2012 from http://articles.mercola.com/sites/articles/archive/2011/07/02/new-study-finds-doctors-are-massively-overprescribing-drugs.aspx

Mercola. (2011, June, 18). A Third of Americans Dont Sleep 7 Hours. Retrieved January 18, 2012, from http://articles.mercola.com/sites/articles/archive/2011/06/18/a-third-of-americans-dont-sleep-7-hoours.aspx

Mercola. (2011, June, 9). Average drug label lists over whopping 70 side effects. Retrieved January 18, 2012, from http://articles.mercola.com/sites/articles/archive/2011/06/09/average-drug-label-lists-over-whopping-70-side-effects.aspx

Mercola. (2011, May 25). This common OTC painkiller found linked to cancer. Retrieved January 30, 2012, from http:articles.mercola.com/sites/articles/archive/2011/05/25/this-common-otc-painkiller-found-linked-to-cancer.aspx

Mercola. (2009, September 26). Pfizer to pay record 2.3 billion dollar fine. Retiived January 30, 2012, from http://articles.

mercola.com/sites/articles/archive/2009/09/26/Pfizer-to-pay-record-23-billion-fine.aspx

Mercola. (2008, December 9). The dangers of taking more than one medication at once. Retrieved February 9, 2012, from http://articles.mercola.com/sites/articles/archive/2008/12/09/the-dangers-of-taking-more-than-one-medication-at-once.aspx

Mercola. (2008, July 3). Why is the US spending more than $1 Trillion for Drugs. Retrieved January 30, 2012, from http://articles.mercola.com/sites/articles/archive/2008/07/03/why-is-the-u-s-spending-more-than-1-trillion-for-drugs.aspx

Mercola. (2006, September 16). Vioxx cousin celebrex also found to cause heart attacks. Retrieved January 30, 2012, from http://articles.mercolacom/sites/articles/archive/2006/09/16/vioxx-cousin-celebrex-slso-found-to-cause-heart-attackes.aspx

Naziroglu, M; Ozgul, C; Cig, B; Dogan, S, Uguz, AC. Glutathione modulates Ca (2+) influx and oxidative toxicity through PTPMZ channel in rat dorsal root ganglion neurons. The Journal of membrane biology. 2011 Aug; 242 (3): 109-18.

Null, G. (2010). *Death By Medicine*. Mount Jackson: Praktikos Books.

Peet, M. (2004). Diet, diabetes, and schizophrenia: review and hypothesis. British Journal of Psychiatry, 184, 381-382.

Plotnikoff, GA, Quigley, JM. Prevalence of severe hypovitaminosis D in patients with persistent, nonspecific musculoskeletal pain. Mayo Clinic Proceedings. 2003 Dec; 78 (12):1463-70.

Pruss, 2007. A patient with cerebral Whipple disease with gastric involvement but no gastrointestinal symptoms: a consequence of local protective immunity? Aug; 78 (8) 896-8.

Robbins, J. (2008). *A Symphony In The Brain*. New York: Grove Press.

Rubio-Tapia, 2009. Increased prevalence and mortality in undiagnosed celiac disease. Gastroenterlogy, 137 (1) 88-93.

Thompson, ME, Barkhuizen, A. Fibromyalgia, hepatitis C infection, and the cytokine connection. Current Pain Headache Reports. 2003 Oct; 7(5): 342-7.

WebMD. (2007, March, 05). Steroid shots for back pain dont work. Retrieved June 22, 2011, from http://webmd.com/back-pain/news/20070305/steroid-shots-for-back-pain-dont-work.

Wilhem, SM; Johnson, JL; Kale-Pradhan, PB, 2011. Treating bugs with bugs: the role of probiotics as adjunctive therapy for Heliobacter pylori. The Annals of pharmacotherapy. 2011 Jul: 45 (7-8): 960-6.

Resources

Drjeremymartin.com- My office website. We are constantly putting new information and updates about various aspects of health. Feel free to contact us with questions.

Mercola.com- One of the most popular natural healthcare websites. A great source of information.

ADHDBeyondthemeds.com- Our website on ADHD.

CPSIA information can be obtained at www.ICGtesting.com
Printed in the USA
LVOW050341030712

288594LV00003B/4/P